Lieber Comic-Fan,

offensichtlich lieben Sie – wie Superman – Herausforderungen und wollen die Abenteuer des Superhelden im amerikanischen Original lesen. Sie werden Ihre Entscheidung nicht bereuen, denn mit den spannenden Geschichten frischen Sie auf unterhaltsame Weise Ihre Englischkenntnisse auf.

Damit Ihr Lesevergnügen nicht durch das Nachschlagen von unbekannten Wörtern beeinträchtigt wird, enthält dieser Comic-Band in regelmäßigen Abständen Ausklappseiten, auf denen Sie die deutschen Übersetzungen der wichtigsten englischen Wörter und Wendungen finden. Neben den englischen Vokabeln ist in eckigen Klammern die Aussprache in vereinfachter Lautschrift angegeben. Die erklärten Wörter beziehungsweise Textstellen sind in den Sprechblasen blau hervorgehoben. Die erste Ausklappseite finden Sie auf Seite 11. Klappen Sie sie einfach nach außen, und werfen Sie immer dann einen Blick darauf, wenn Sie auf ein Wort stoßen, das Sie nicht kennen.

Sollten Sie trotz der Vokabelerklärungen bei manchen Geschichten den Faden verlieren, dann lassen Sie sich nicht entmutigen: Auf den Seiten 115–117 finden Sie zu jedem Superman-Abenteuer eine kurze Inhaltsangabe, die Ihnen auf die Sprünge hilft.

Vielleicht haben Sie nach dem Lesen der Geschichten Spaß daran, Ihren Lernfortschritt zu überprüfen. Zu den einzelnen Episoden bieten wir Ihnen auf den Seiten 118–128 Kreuzwort- und Buchstabenrätsel sowie eine Reihe anderer kniffliger Aufgaben an. Durch die erneute Verwendung der Vokabeln werden sie noch besser im Gedächtnis verankert – und Sie können später leichter darauf zurückgreifen. Selbstverständlich sind auch die entsprechenden Lösungen im Anhang abgedruckt.

Viel Spaß beim Lesen!

Hinweise zur vereinfachten Lautschrift

Damit die Aussprache leicht nachvollziehbar ist, wurden bei dieser Lautschrift – von wenigen Ausnahmen abgesehen – Buchstaben aus dem deutschen Alphabet verwendet. Diese werden so ausgesprochen, wie Sie es vom Deutschen her gewohnt sind.
Einige Besonderheiten sollten Sie aber beachten:

[ə]	arrive [əraiv]	gesprochen wie das kurze, unbetonte *e* in *bitte*
[ð]	the [ðə]	Das *th* wird wie ein stimmhaftes gelispeltes *s* in *Hase* gesprochen.
[θ]	three [θrih]	Das *th* wird wie ein stimmloses gelispeltes *s* in *Faß* gesprochen.
[v]	very [veri]	wie *w* in *wenig*
[w]	wine [wain]	wie *u* und *w* schnell hintereinander gesprochen
[s]	pleased [plihsd]	stimmhaft, weich gesprochen wie *s* in *sehen*
[ß]	street [ßtriht]	stimmlos, gesprochen wie *s* in *das* oder *ß* in *Straße*
[ai]	five [faiv]	wie *ei* in *mein* oder *ai* in *Main*
[äi]	say [ßäi]	*ä* und *i* schnell hintereinander gesprochen
[ou]	home [houm]	*o* und *u* schnell hintereinander gesprochen
[h]	student [ßtuhdnt]	hinter einem Vokal: lang gesprochen wie in *Stuhl*
	hand [händ]	vor einem Vokal: wie *h* in *haben*
ˈ	bedeutet, dass die nachfolgende Silbe betont ausgesprochen werden soll.	

Berlitz®

Englisch lernen mit Superman™

Up, up and away!

Superman created by Jerry Siegel and Joe Shuster

Berlitz Publishing
München · New York · Singapur

Berlitz Englisch lernen mit Superman™ – Up, up and away!

Vokabelerklärungen und Übungen: Astrid Stannat
Projektleitung: Eva Betz

www.dccomics.com
www.berlitzpublishing.de

Berlitz Publishing
Mies-van-der-Rohe-Straße 1
D-80807 München

Printed in Austria
ISBN 978-3-468-79406-3

2. 3. 4. 5   11 10 09 08 07

CLARK KENT, YOU'RE A NOBODY!
MAYDAY! MAYDAY! METROPOLIS TOWER,
WE'VE BEEN HIT! WE'VE BEEN HIT! REQUEST EMERGENCY LANDING!
LEXAIR
MARK MILLAR - WRITER
ALUIR AMANCIO - PENCILLER
TERRY AUSTIN - INKER
LOIS BUHALIS - LETTERER
RICK TAYLOR - COLORIST
MAUREEN MCTIGUE - ASSISTANT
MIKE MCAVENNIE - EDITOR
SUPERMAN CREATED BY JERRY SIEGEL AND JOE SHUSTER

SOMETHING WRONG, Mr. KENT?
THE PLANET'S COMPUTERS HAVE BEEN DOWN ALL MORNING, JIMMY. MY DIARY'S LOST IN HERE SOMEWHERE, AND I'M SURE SOMETHING IMPORTANT WAS HAPPENING TODAY.
I JUST CAN'T FIGURE OUT WHAT.
COULD BE AN APPOINTMENT WITH YOUR OPTICIAN.
MISS LANE SAYS YOU'VE BEEN WANDERING AROUND THE OFFICE LIKE MISTER MAGOO FOR WEEKS.
Oh, MY GOD!
A PASSENGER JET JUST COLLIDED WITH A SMALLER PLANE!
IT CAN'T REACH THE AIRPORT IN TIME AND THE POLICE ARE CLEARING A STREET FOR THEM TO LAND!
AT LUNCHTIME? THEY DON'T HAVE A CHANCE! IF ONLY THERE WERE SOME WAY WE COULD CONTACT SUPERMAN!
ANY IDEAS, Mr. KENT?
Mr. KENT?
WHERE'D HE GO?

WELL, AS THE SAYING GOES...
"THIS LOOKS LIKE A JOB FOR--
--SUPERMAN?"
AAAAHH!
--I-I DON'T BELIEVE IT!
I CAN'T FLY!
I CAN'T FLY!!

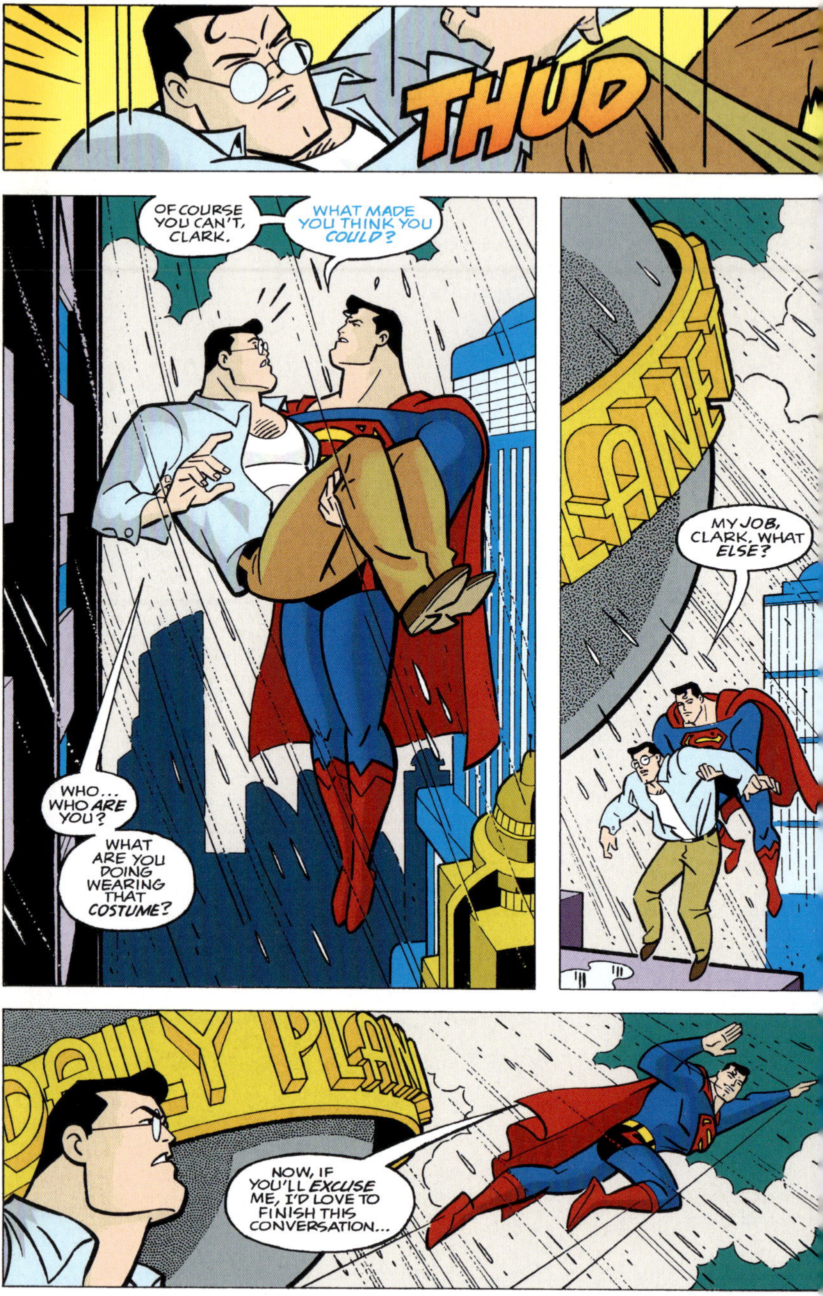
THUD
OF COURSE YOU CAN'T, CLARK.
WHAT MADE YOU THINK YOU COULD?
WHO... WHO ARE YOU?
WHAT ARE YOU DOING WEARING THAT COSTUME?
MY JOB, CLARK. WHAT ELSE?
NOW, IF YOU'LL EXCUSE ME, I'D LOVE TO FINISH THIS CONVERSATION...

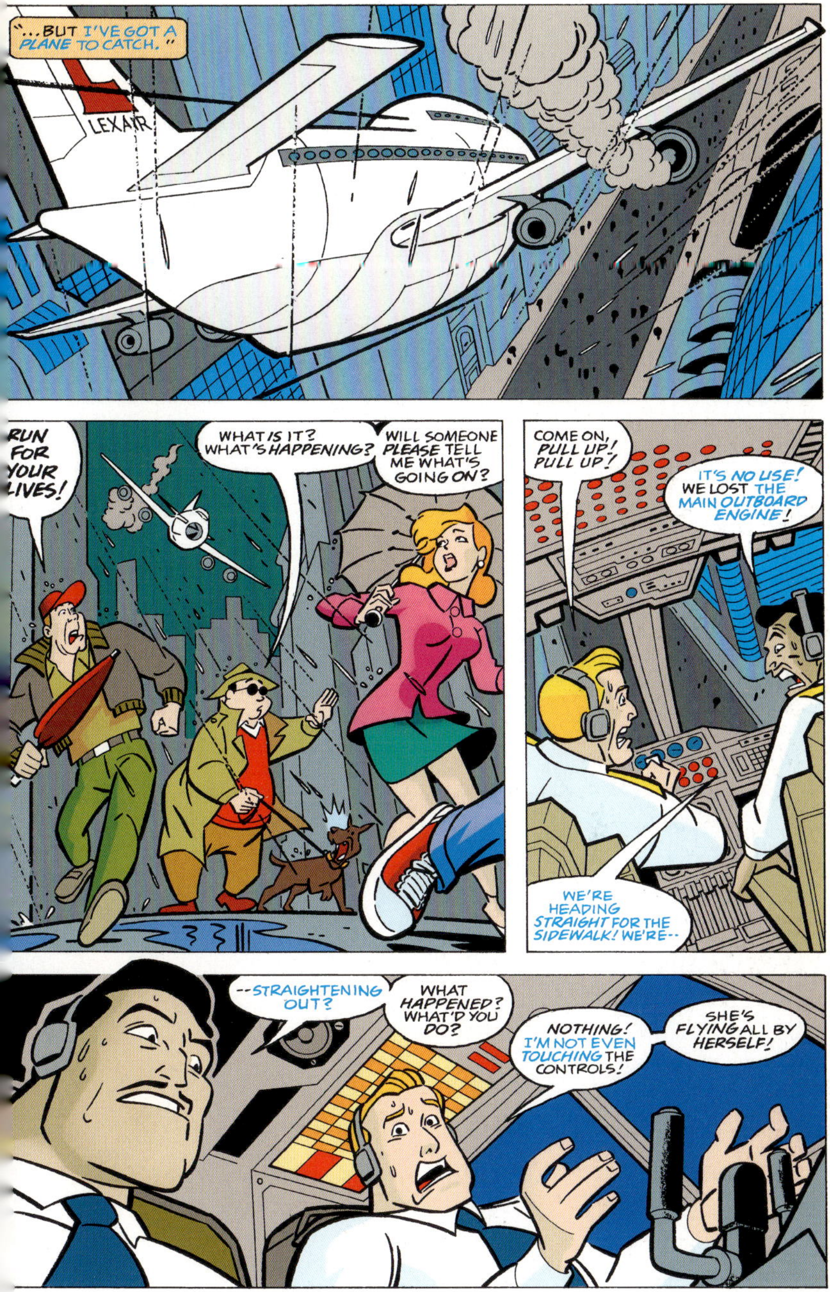

"...BUT I'VE GOT A PLANE TO CATCH."
LEXAIR
RUN FOR YOUR LIVES!
WHAT IS IT? WHAT'S HAPPENING?
WILL SOMEONE PLEASE TELL ME WHAT'S GOING ON?
COME ON, PULL UP! PULL UP!
IT'S NO USE! WE LOST THE MAIN OUTBOARD ENGINE!
WE'RE HEADING STRAIGHT FOR THE SIDEWALK! WE'RE--
--STRAIGHTENING OUT?
WHAT HAPPENED? WHAT'D YOU DO?
NOTHING! I'M NOT EVEN TOUCHING THE CONTROLS!
SHE'S FLYING ALL BY HERSELF!

WHERE ARE YOU HEADED?
NOT EXACTLY, SIR.
SUPERMAN! THANK GOD!
WE'RE DUE TO LAND IN GOTHAM CITY IN ABOUT TWENTY MINUTES, SUPERMAN! CAN YOU HEAR ME OKAY OUT THERE?
OF COURSE HE CAN. HE'S GOT SUPER-HEARING...
FASTEN YOUR SAFETY-BELTS, GENTLEMEN!
I'LL HAVE YOU THERE IN TEN!
INCREDIBLE...
WHAT'S THE MATTER, SMALLVILLE? LIFE IN THE BIG CITY GETTING TOO EXCITING FOR YOU?

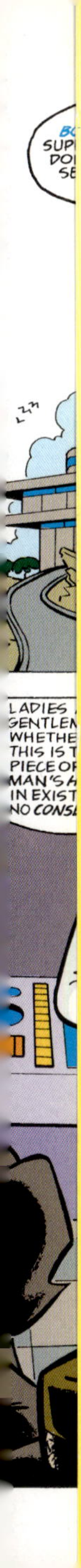

Vokabelerklärungen (S. 12–21)

S. 12/13
harmful to the environment [ˈhahrmful tə ði inˈvairənment] umweltschädlich
however you dispose of it [hauˈevər ju dißˈpous əv it] wie auch immer Sie sie entsorgen
precaution [priˈkahschən] Vorsichtsmaßnahme
impostor [imˈpahstər] Betrüger
drained [dräind] erschöpft
gust of [gaßt əv] Hauch von
orphans [ˈohrfəns] Waisenkinder
responsibly [riˈßpahnßəbli] verantwortungsbewusst
homicidal maniac [hahməˈßaidl ˈmäiniäk] Amokläufer
villain [ˈvilən] Schurke
Buddy, could you spare a dime? [ˈbadi kud ju ßper ə daim] Kumpel, hast du vielleicht zehn Cent übrig?

S. 14/15
streetwise [ˈßtrihtwais] gewieft
wallet [ˈwahlət] Brieftasche
We're in charge here! [wir in tschardsch hir] Wir haben hier das Sagen!
Good grief! [gud grihf] Großer Gott!
Just a few cuts and bruises. [dschaßt ə fjuh katß ənd ˈbruhsis] Nur ein paar Schnittwunden und Prellungen.
under the circumstances [ˈandər ðə ˈßörkəmßtänßis] unter diesen Umständen

S. 16/17
removes every trace [riˈmuhvs ˈevri träiß] beseitigt jede Spur
vault [vahlt] Tresor
spare [ßper] Ersatz-
they're teaming up [ðäir ˈtihming ap] sie tun sich zusammen
combined assault [kamˈbaind əˈßahlt] gemeinsamer Angriff
when I've been stripped of my powers [wen aiv bin ßtript əv mai ˈpauərs] wenn ich meiner Kräfte beraubt worden bin
Clark's only teasing you [klarkß ˈounli ˈtihsing ju] Clark nimmt dich nur auf den Arm
scorched [ßkortscht] verbrannt
delusion [diˈluhschən] Wahnvorstellung
face reality [fäiß riˈäliti] der Realität ins Auge sehen

S. 18/19
air currents [er ˈkarəntß] Luftströmungen
unwind [anˈwaind] auflösen/entwirren
in tarnation [in tarˈnäischn] verdammt

S. 20/21
hunch [hantsch] Ahnung
Jurassic age [dschuˈräßik äidsch] Jurazeitalter

► *Nächste Ausklappseite: S. 31*

IS IT POSSIBLE SUCH A HIGHLY-RADIOACTIVE SUBSTANCE WILL BE HARMFUL TO THE ENVIRONMENT HOWEVER YOU DISPOSE OF IT, PROFESSOR HAMILTON?
BELIEVE ME, MISTER KENT, S.T.A.R. HAS TAKEN EVERY POSSIBLE PRECAUTION.
WOULD TOUCHING IT HAVE ANY EFFECT ON ME?
HaHaHaHaHa!
NOT UNLESS YOU COME FROM KRYPTON.
MAY I?
SIGH IF IT SELLS NEWSPAPERS, Mr. KENT.
NO EFFECT! THIS IS WORSE THAN I THOUGHT.
NOT ONLY HAS THIS IMPOSTOR ROBBED ME OF MY POWERS, I'VE BEEN TURNED INTO AN ORDINARY HUMAN BEING!
YOU OKAY, KENT?
I'M FINE, LOIS.
THAT'S THE PROBLEM.

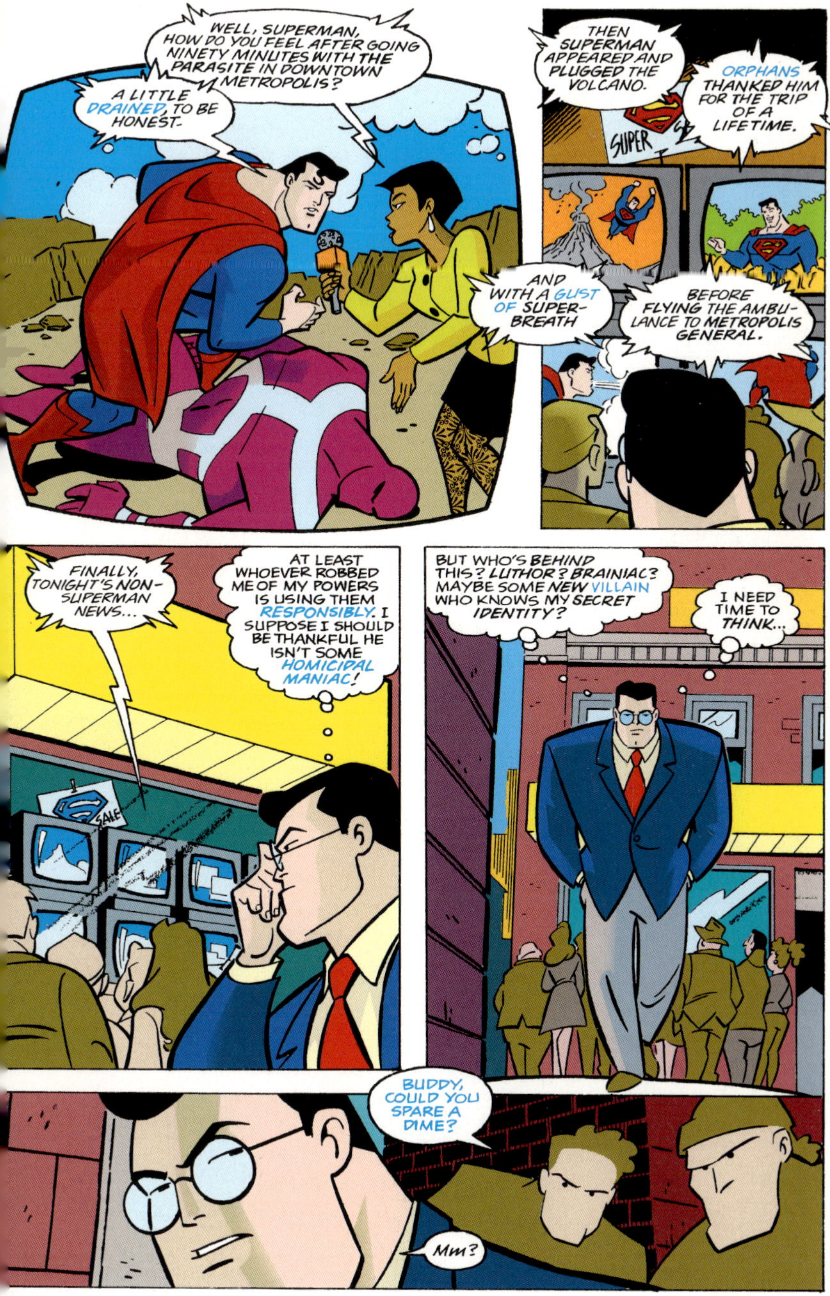
WELL, SUPERMAN, HOW DO YOU FEEL AFTER GOING NINETY MINUTES WITH THE PARASITE IN DOWNTOWN METROPOLIS?
A LITTLE DRAINED, TO BE HONEST-
THEN SUPERMAN APPEARED AND PLUGGED THE VOLCANO.
ORPHANS THANKED HIM FOR THE TRIP OF A LIFETIME.
SUPER
AND WITH A GUST OF SUPER-BREATH
BEFORE FLYING THE AMBU-LANCE TO METROPOLIS GENERAL.
FINALLY, TONIGHT'S NON-SUPERMAN NEWS...
AT LEAST WHOEVER ROBBED ME OF MY POWERS IS USING THEM RESPONSIBLY. I SUPPOSE I SHOULD BE THANKFUL HE ISN'T SOME HOMICIDAL MANIAC!
SALE
BUT WHO'S BEHIND THIS? LUTHOR? BRAINIAC? MAYBE SOME NEW VILLAIN WHO KNOWS MY SECRET IDENTITY?
I NEED TIME TO THINK...
BUDDY, COULD YOU SPARE A DIME?
Mm?

WHUD
SORRY! I MEANT TO SAY GIVE ME EVERYTHING YOU'VE GOT OR WE SHOOT YOU IN THE HEAD!
A NEWSPAPER REPORTER? YOU'D THINK SOMEONE IN YOUR LINE OF WORK'D BE A LITTLE MORE STREETWISE!
LISTEN, I DON'T WANT ANY TROUBLE.
JUST TAKE THE WALLET AND GO.
KRAKK!
UNNH!
SHUT UP! WE'RE IN CHARGE HERE!
YOU DON'T EVEN SPEAK!
HEY, I GOT AN IDEA...
LET'S GIVE 'IM SOMETHIN' WORTH WRITIN' ABOUT IN HIS NEWSPAPER!
SUPERMAN SAYS: HELP STAMP OUT CRIME
WHOK!
THUD!
SOK!

HEY! WHAT'S GOING ON OVER THERE?!
HAHAHA HAHAHAHA
GOOD GRIEF!
MY GLASSES...CAN'T SEE WITHOUT MY GLASSES...
YOU'RE GOING TO BE FINE, MISTER. JUST A FEW CUTS AND BRUISES. NOTHING TO GET WORKED UP ABOUT.
SAY... I KNOW THIS PROBABLY SOUNDS KIND OF STRANGE UNDER THE CIRCUMSTANCES...
...BUT HAS ANYONE EVER MENTIONED YOU LOOK A LOT LIKE SUPERMAN WITHOUT YOUR GLASSES?
I HARDLY KNOW WHERE TO START, PA...

FIRST, SOME UNKNOWN QUANTITY STEALS MY COSTUME AND POWERS. THEN SOMEONE REMOVES EVERY TRACE OF MY SUPERMAN CAREER FROM THE VAULT IN MY APARTMENT.
EVEN THE SPARE COSTUMES AND ALIEN SOUVENIRS.
THE MOST OBVIOUS ANSWER IS THAT ONE OF MY ENEMIES HAS FIGURED OUT MY SECRET IDENTITY. MAYBE ALL OF THEM HAVE, AND THEY'RE TEAMING UP FOR A COMBINED ASSAULT.
BUT HOW DO I FIGHT THEM WHEN I'VE BEEN STRIPPED OF MY POWERS? WHAT AM I SUPPOSED TO DO NEXT?
JONATHAN? WHAT'S HE SAYING?
EASY, MARTHA. CLARK'S ONLY TEASING YOU WITH ALL THIS SUPERMAN NONSENSE. ISN'T THAT RIGHT, SON?
TELL YOUR MA YOU AREN'T SERIOUS.
AM I... AM I LOSING MY MIND?

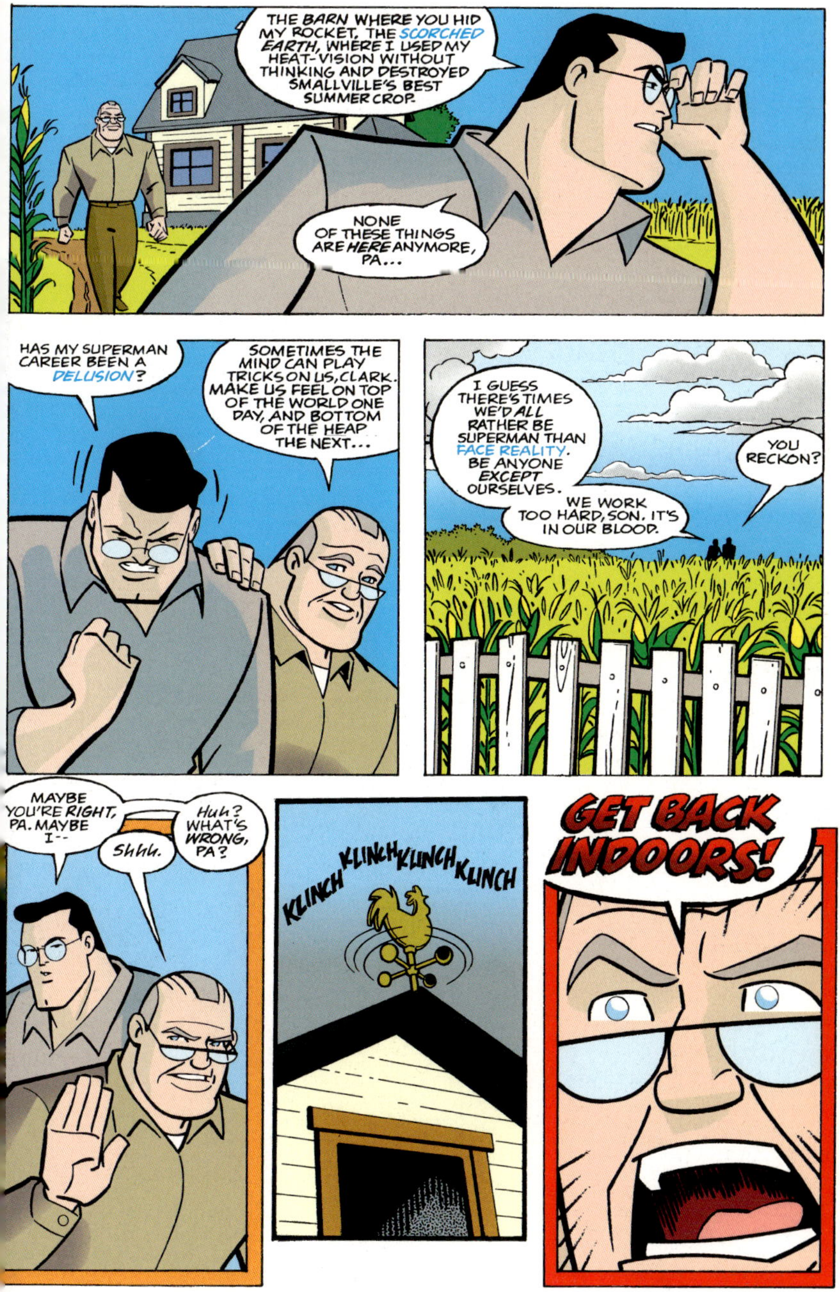

THE BARN WHERE YOU HID MY ROCKET, THE SCORCHED EARTH, WHERE I USED MY HEAT-VISION WITHOUT THINKING AND DESTROYED SMALLVILLE'S BEST SUMMER CROP.
NONE OF THESE THINGS ARE HERE ANYMORE, PA...
HAS MY SUPERMAN CAREER BEEN A DELUSION?
SOMETIMES THE MIND CAN PLAY TRICKS ON US, CLARK. MAKE US FEEL ON TOP OF THE WORLD ONE DAY, AND BOTTOM OF THE HEAP THE NEXT...
I GUESS THERE'S TIMES WE'D ALL RATHER BE SUPERMAN THAN FACE REALITY. BE ANYONE EXCEPT OURSELVES.
YOU RECKON?
WE WORK TOO HARD, SON. IT'S IN OUR BLOOD.
MAYBE YOU'RE RIGHT, PA. MAYBE I--
Shhh.
Huh? WHAT'S WRONG, PA?
KLINCH KLINCH KLINCH KLINCH
GET BACK INDOORS!

GREAT SCOTT!
GET UNDER THE HOUSE, CLARK!
IT'S A TWISTER!
CLARK!

SORRY ABOUT THE TRACTOR, FOLKS.
I'LL STOP BY AND REPAIR IT LATER.
NOW PLEASE TAKE COVER!
CLARK! ARE YOU ALL RIGHT, SON?
I... I DON'T KNOW ANYMORE, PA.
WHAT'S HE GOING TO DO?
FIGURE OUT WHICH WAY THE AIR CURRENTS ARE MOVING AND UNWIND THE TORNADO IN THE OPPOSITE DIRECTION.
"HOW IN TARNATION DID YOU KNOW THAT, CLARK?"

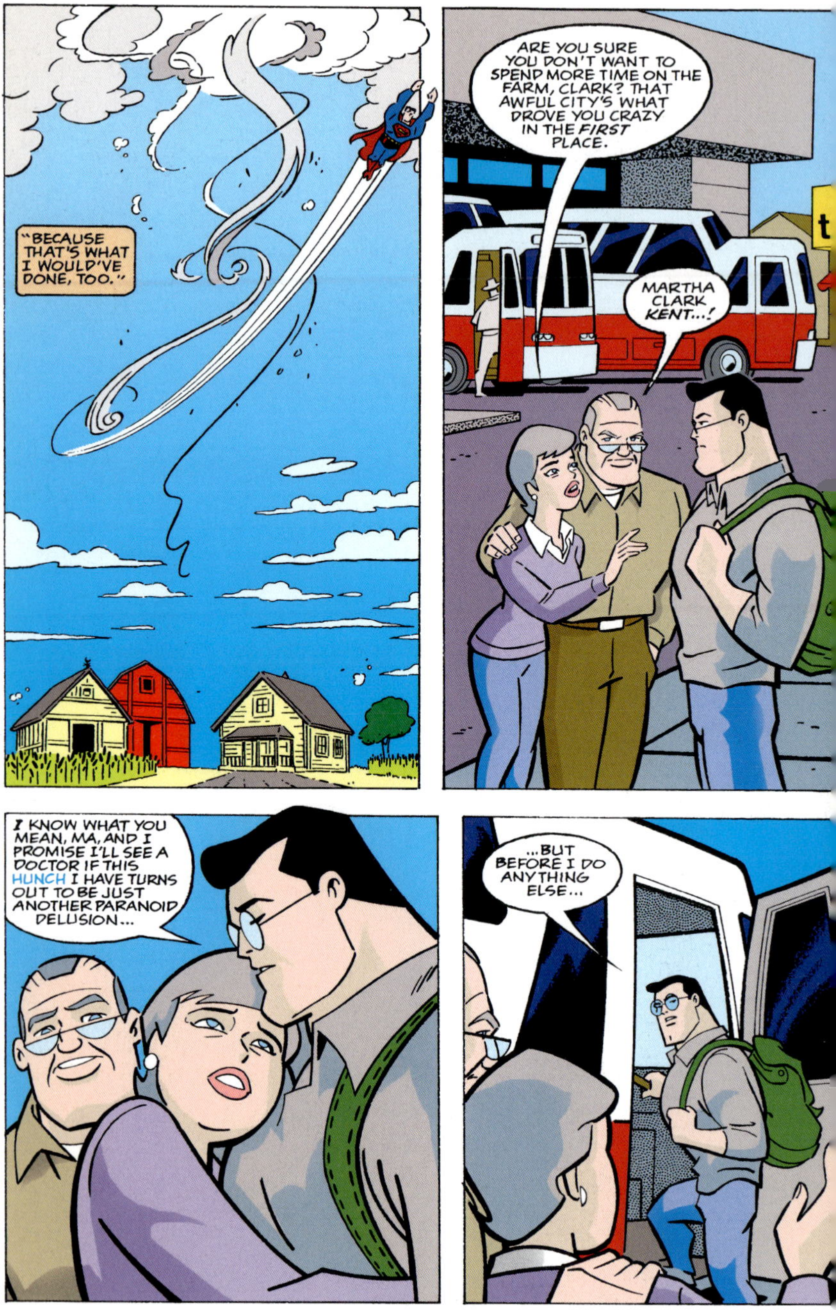
"BECAUSE THAT'S WHAT I WOULD'VE DONE, TOO."
ARE YOU SURE YOU DON'T WANT TO SPEND MORE TIME ON THE FARM, CLARK? THAT AWFUL CITY'S WHAT DROVE YOU CRAZY IN THE *FIRST* PLACE.
MARTHA CLARK *KENT*...!
I KNOW WHAT YOU MEAN, MA, AND I PROMISE I'LL SEE A DOCTOR IF THIS HUNCH I HAVE TURNS OUT TO BE JUST ANOTHER PARANOID DELUSION...
...BUT BEFORE I DO ANYTHING ELSE...

"...THERE'S SOMETHING I HAVE TO CHECK FIRST."
WE ONLY CAME BACK ON-LINE THIS MORNING, Mr. KENT.
THE LAST COUPLE OF DAYS FELT LIKE WE WERE PUTTING TOGETHER A NEWSPAPER IN THE JURASSIC AGE.
ANY LUCK FINDING YOUR DIARY MESSAGES?
COMING RIGHT UP, JIMMY...
TODAY'S THE DAY
MESSAGE TO BE REPEATED EVERY NINETY DAYS
OF COURSE!
SNAP
I TAKE IT THIS IS GOOD NEWS?
"THE BEST."
UNBELIEVABLE!
WHEET WHEET WHEET WHEET WHEET WHEET WHEET WHEET WHEET WHEET WHEET

WHEETWHEETWHEET
YOU DON'T NEED TO INSULT ME IN MORSE-CODE USING A SILENT DOG WHISTLE TO GET MY ATTENTION, CLARK.
THERE ARE MORE POLITE WAYS OF GETTING IN TOUCH.
YOU CAN DROP THE ACT. NOBODY'S FOOLED FOR A SECOND.
YOU'RE NOT SUPERMAN.
I'M THE REAL SUPERMAN, AND I CAN PROVE IT.
WHAT WILL IT BE THIS TIME, CLARK? JUMPING OFF THE ROOF OF THE DAILY PLANET IN A CAPE AND TIGHTS?
YOU NEED TO SEE A PSYCHIATRIST!
ANYONE CAN WEAR THAT RIDICULOUS OUTFIT. I WANT TO SEE SOME HARD FACTS!

YOU *SURE* ABOUT THAT?
SO YOU CAN FLY. DOZENS OF SUPER-HUMANS ON THIS PLANET CAN FLY.
WHAT *ELSE* CAN YOU DO?
ANYTHING.
I CAN HEAR MILK TURNING TO CHEESE, READ NEWSPAPER HEADLINES IN GOTHAM, SMELL KETCHUP ON A BURGER TEN CITY BLOCKS FROM HERE...

I CAN DO ANYTHING.
WHAT CAN YOU DO?
WHAT ABOUT X-RAY VISION? EVERYONE KNOWS ONLY SUPERMAN HAS X-RAY VISION. READ THE ENVELOPE IN MY BREAST POCKET AND YOU'LL HAVE ME CONVINCED.
PIECE OF CAKE.
"BRAINIAC. LUTHOR. KLTPZYXM. KLTPZYXM. PARASITE..."
THERE. NOW DO YOU--?
OOPS.
JUST AS I SUSPECTED. HELLO...
POOF!

...Mr. MXYZPTLK!
HOW DID YOU KNOW IT WAS ME?
TELL ME! TELL ME BEFORE I DISAPPEAR!
YOU'RE A FIFTH-DIMENSIONAL IMP WHO CAN VISIT THIS WORLD EVERY NINETY DAYS, MXYZPTLK.
I HAVE TO TAKE PRECAUTIONS WHEN I'M DEALING WITH SOMEONE WHO CAN BEND REALITY AND UPSET TIME AND SPACE THE WAY YOU CAN...
"MY E-MAIL MESSAGES WERE REMINDERS THAT NINETY DAYS HAD PASSED AND YOU WERE FREE TO CAUSE TROUBLE AGAIN.
"AT LEAST UNTIL I FIGURED OUT SOME WAY TO MAKE YOU SAY YOUR NAME BACKWARDS TWICE AND--"
I KNOW. I KNOW! SEND ME BACK TO THE FIFTH DIMENSION FOR ANOTHER NINETY DAYS!
JUST WAIT TILL NEXT TIME, MORON! JUST YOU WAIT
POOF!
CATCH YOU LATER, MXYZPTLK.
DON'T HURRY BACK.

WELL, NOW THAT THAT'S SETTLED...
CALLING ALL UNITS! CALLING ALL UNITS!
THE TOYMAN AND A HUNDRED ARMED ACTION FIGURES ARE ROBBING THE JEWELRY EMPORIUM OFF BATES AND MAGGIN!
PLEASE ATTEND! PLEASE ATTEND!
LOOK! UP IN THE SKY!
IT'S A BIRD!
IT'S A PLANE!
THESE TOURISTS DRIVE ME CRAZY...
IT'S SUPERMAN!
The End

THE BODYGUARD of STEEL
"DON'T WORRY, MISTER PRESIDENT. THIS IS AS CLOSE AS SUPERMAN GETS TO THE WHITE HOUSE..."
MARK MILLAR - WRITER
ALUIR AMANCIO - PENCILLER
TERRY AUSTIN - INKER
RICK TAYLOR - COLORIST
LOIS BUHALIS - LETTERER
FRANK BERRIOS - ASSISTANT
MIKE McAVENNIE - EDITOR
SUPERMAN CREATED BY JERRY SIEGEL & JOE SHUSTER

"OUR BOYS HAVE ENOUGH FIREPOWER OUT THERE TO LEVEL THE STATE. I PROMISE HE WON'T GET ANYWHERE NEAR US."
"THAT'S NOT HOW THINGS LOOK FROM WHERE I'M SITTING, GENERAL HARDCASTLE..."
WHOOOOMM!
"THE LEXCORP GROUND-TO AIR MISSILE SYSTEM WAS ONLY OUR FIRST LINE OF DEFENSE, SIR. THE ENTIRE BUILDING IS SURROUNDED BY HIGHLY-DECORATED NAVY SEALS...
FWOOSH!
FWOOSH!
"...EVEN IF HE MANAGES TO GET PAST THEM, THE NEW WHITE HOUSE EXTERIOR WE DESIGNED IS STRONG ENOUGH TO WITHSTAND THE EFFECTS OF A LOCALIZED NUCLEAR BLAST.
"THIS IS DEFINITELY AS FAR AS HE GOES..."

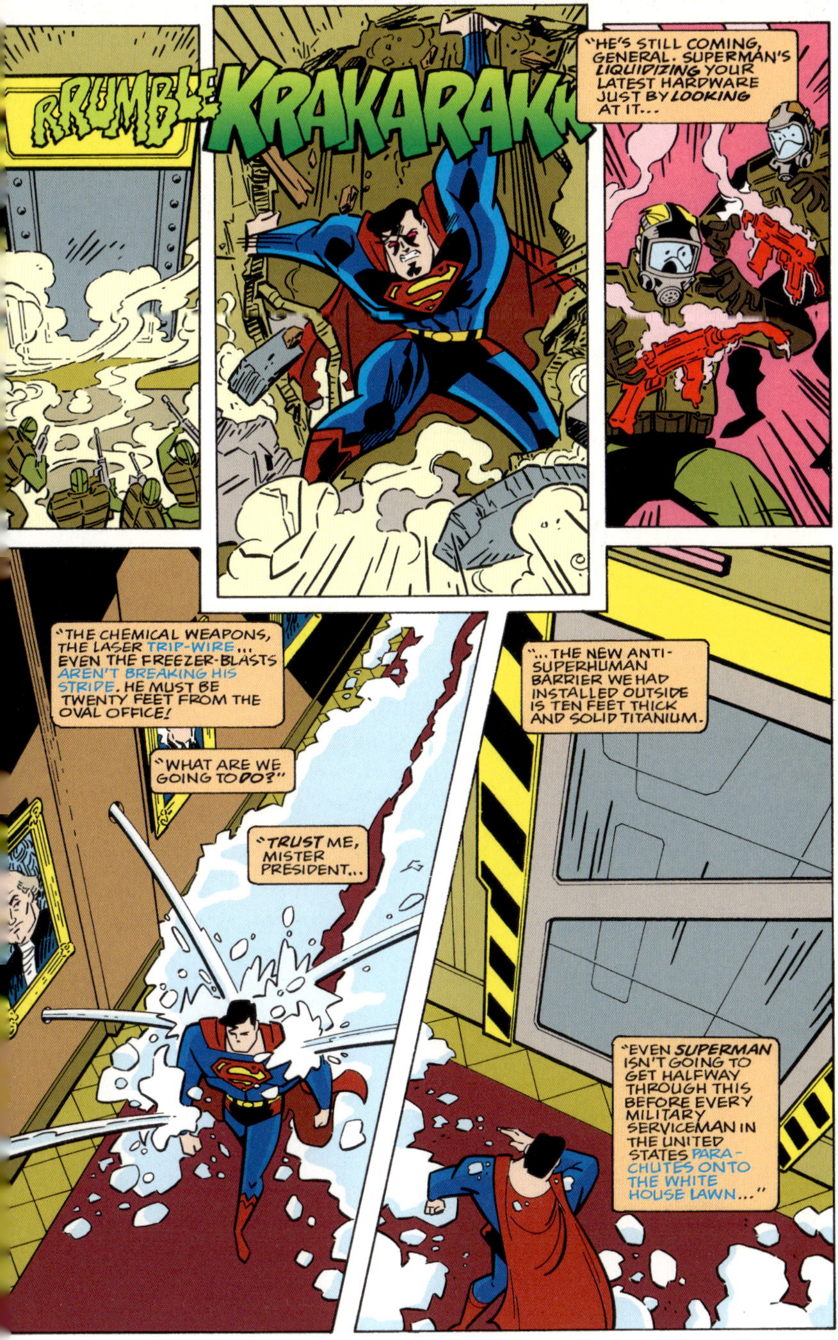
RRUMBLE
KRAKARAKK
"HE'S STILL COMING, GENERAL. SUPERMAN'S LIQUIDIZING YOUR LATEST HARDWARE JUST BY LOOKING AT IT...
"THE CHEMICAL WEAPONS, THE LASER TRIP-WIRE... EVEN THE FREEZER-BLASTS AREN'T BREAKING HIS STRIDE. HE MUST BE TWENTY FEET FROM THE OVAL OFFICE!
"WHAT ARE WE GOING TO DO?"
"TRUST ME, MISTER PRESIDENT...
"...THE NEW ANTI-SUPERHUMAN BARRIER WE HAD INSTALLED OUTSIDE IS TEN FEET THICK AND SOLID TITANIUM.
"EVEN SUPERMAN ISN'T GOING TO GET HALFWAY THROUGH THIS BEFORE EVERY MILITARY SERVICEMAN IN THE UNITED STATES PARA-CHUTES ONTO THE WHITE HOUSE LAWN..."

WE'VE GOT MORE THAN ENOUGH TIME TO GET YOU OUT OF HERE IN OUR SPECIALLY-DESIGNED ESCAPE POD.
I STILL SAY WE SHOULD'VE MADE MORE OF AN EFFORT TO LOCATE A DECENT PIECE OF KRYPTONITE. BUT THE SITUATION IS NOT UNSATISFACTORY, MISTER PRESIDENT.
UH, GENERAL...
...SUPERMAN JUST DISAPPEARED FROM THE SCREEN.
WHAT?!
SECTOR
HE'S IN!
THRUNNGH!
BANG, MISTER PRESIDENT.
YOU'RE DEAD.

DAILY PLANET
WHAT DO YOU MEAN YOU NEED A VACATION, KENT?
ONLY FOR A COUPLE OF DAYS, CHIEF.
I COMPLETELY FORGOT ABOUT MY HIGH SCHOOL REUNION. LOIS SAID SHE'D BE MORE THAN HAPPY TO COVER THAT PEACE TREATY ASSIGNMENT WHILE I'M GONE.
WELL, I DON'T LIKE SHUFFLING MY REPORTERS LIKE A DECK OF CARDS, BUT IF LANE RECKONS SHE CAN FIT THIS INTO HER SCHEDULE, I GUESS IT'S OKAY... JUST THIS ONCE.
THANKS, PERRY.
WHAT DO YOU THINK, JIMMY? SMALLVILLE SEEMS A LITTLE TOO EAGER TO GET TIME OFF WORK FOR A SQUARE DANCE.
I'VE GOT A HUNCH THERE'S SOMETHING THE FARM-BOY'S NOT TELLING US HERE.
CAREFUL, LOIS...
...YOU ALMOST SOUNDED JEALOUS FOR A MOMENT.

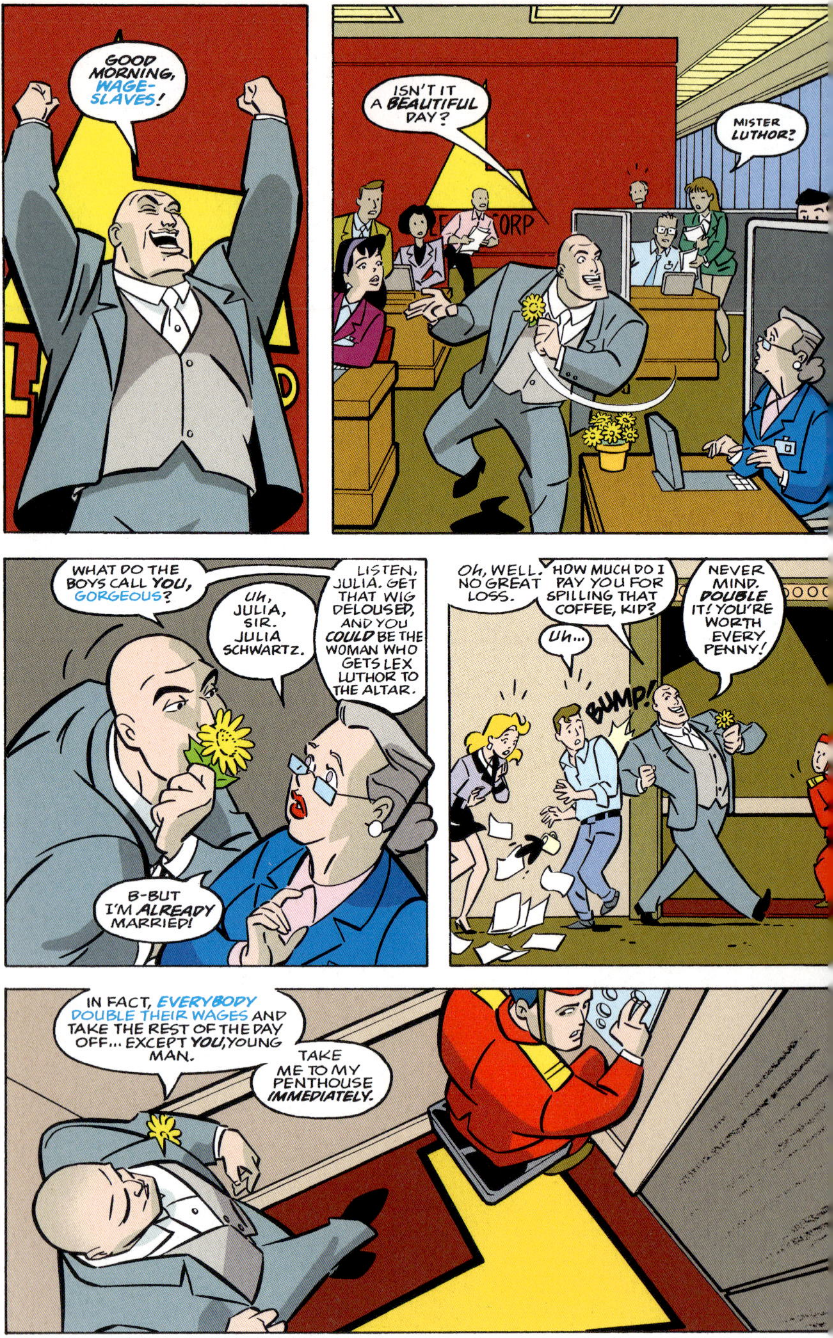
GOOD MORNING, WAGE-SLAVES!
ISN'T IT A BEAUTIFUL DAY?
MISTER LUTHOR?
WHAT DO THE BOYS CALL YOU, GORGEOUS?
Uh, JULIA, SIR. JULIA SCHWARTZ.
LISTEN, JULIA. GET THAT WIG DELOUSED, AND YOU COULD BE THE WOMAN WHO GETS LEX LUTHOR TO THE ALTAR.
B-BUT I'M ALREADY MARRIED!
Oh, WELL. NO GREAT LOSS.
HOW MUCH DO I PAY YOU FOR SPILLING THAT COFFEE, KID?
Uh...
BUMP!
NEVER MIND. DOUBLE IT! YOU'RE WORTH EVERY PENNY!
IN FACT, EVERYBODY DOUBLE THEIR WAGES AND TAKE THE REST OF THE DAY OFF... EXCEPT YOU, YOUNG MAN.
TAKE ME TO MY PENTHOUSE IMMEDIATELY.

I DON'T KNOW WHO YOU THINK YOU'RE FOOLING, MISTER, BUT YOU'D BETTER LEAVE THE BUILDING WHILE I STILL FEEL FRIENDLY ENOUGH TO LET YOU USE THE DOOR.
MERCY, MY DEAR, YOU'RE SO SUSPICIOUS.
HOW COULD AN IMPOSTOR POSSIBLY FAKE A DNA SCAN?
BOSS? I'M SORRY. THOUGHT YOU WERE ALREADY HERE. IT'S JUST THAT I'VE NEVER SEEN YOU QUITE LIKE THIS.
LEX LUTHOR I.D. POSITIVE
DID SUPERMAN GET HIT BY A BOMB OR SOMETHING?
OH, LIGHTEN UP, MERCY.
YOU'RE WAY TOO INTENSE FOR SUCH A CUTE CHICK.
EEP!
Ta-DAAA!
IMPRESSIVE, OR WHAT?
AM I SUPPOSED TO BE IMPRESSED WATCHING YOU DEMOLISH A CAREFULLY CULTIVATED REPUTATION AMONG MY EMPLOYEES?
INCIDENTALLY, THOSE PAY RAISES YOU AWARDED THE LITTLE PEOPLE DOWNSTAIRS WILL BE DEDUCTED FROM YOUR FINAL BILL. I'VE ALREADY DONE THE ARITHMETIC...

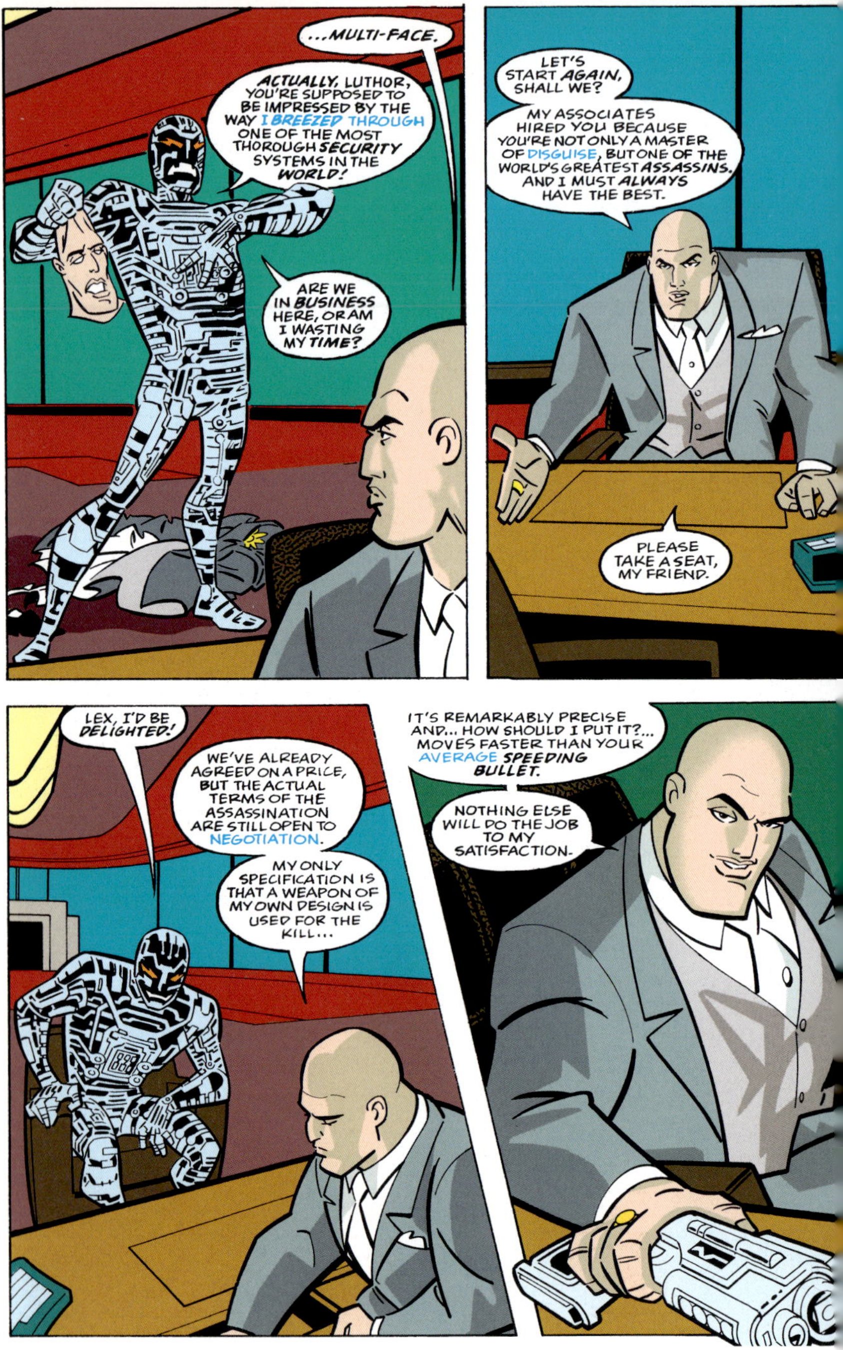
...MULTI-FACE.
ACTUALLY, LUTHOR, YOU'RE SUPPOSED TO BE IMPRESSED BY THE WAY I BREEZED THROUGH ONE OF THE MOST THOROUGH SECURITY SYSTEMS IN THE WORLD!
ARE WE IN BUSINESS HERE, OR AM I WASTING MY TIME?
LET'S START AGAIN, SHALL WE?
MY ASSOCIATES HIRED YOU BECAUSE YOU'RE NOT ONLY A MASTER OF DISGUISE, BUT ONE OF THE WORLD'S GREATEST ASSASSINS. AND I MUST ALWAYS HAVE THE BEST.
PLEASE TAKE A SEAT, MY FRIEND.
LEX, I'D BE DELIGHTED!
WE'VE ALREADY AGREED ON A PRICE, BUT THE ACTUAL TERMS OF THE ASSASSINATION ARE STILL OPEN TO NEGOTIATION.
MY ONLY SPECIFICATION IS THAT A WEAPON OF MY OWN DESIGN IS USED FOR THE KILL...
IT'S REMARKABLY PRECISE AND... HOW SHOULD I PUT IT?... MOVES FASTER THAN YOUR AVERAGE SPEEDING BULLET.
NOTHING ELSE WILL DO THE JOB TO MY SATISFACTION.

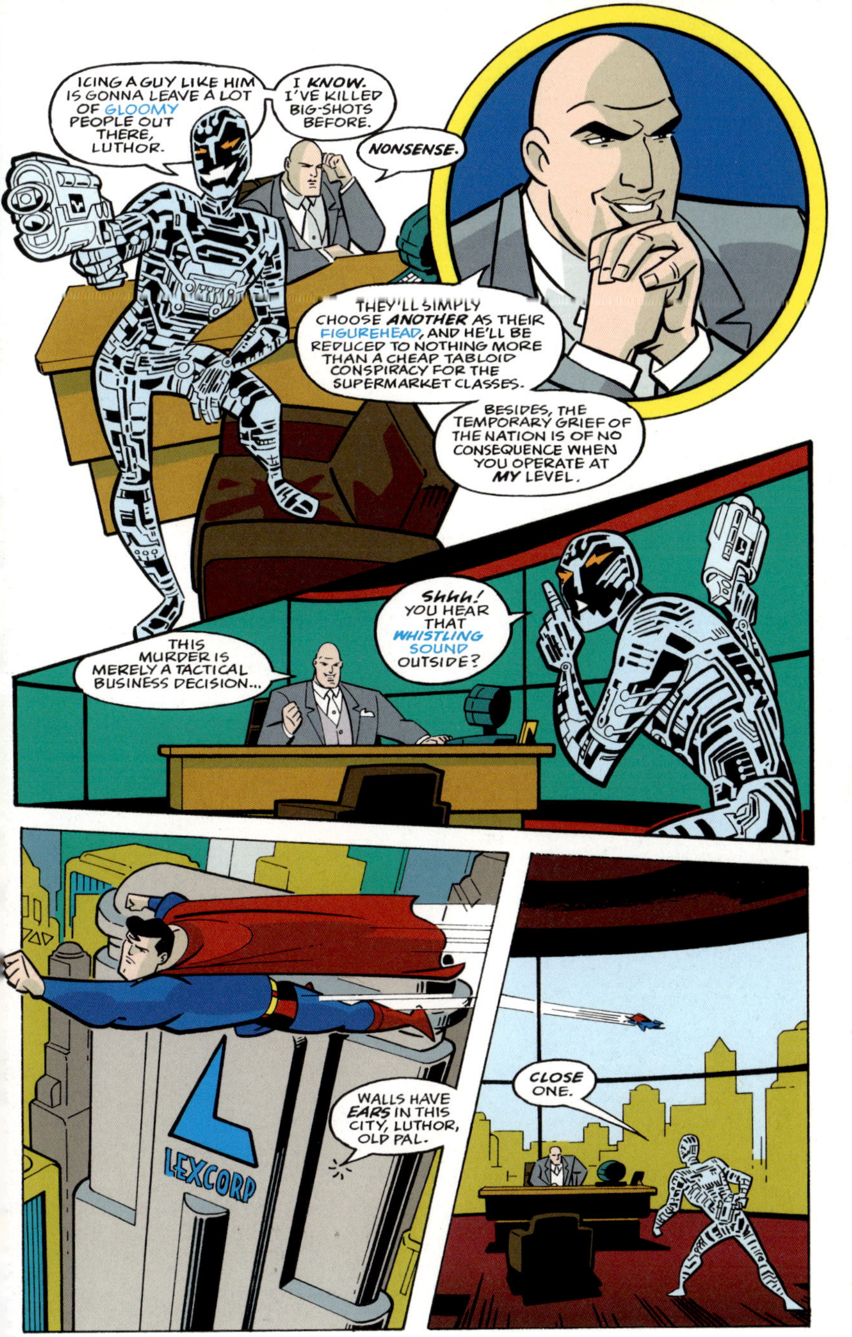
ICING A GUY LIKE HIM IS GONNA LEAVE A LOT OF GLOOMY PEOPLE OUT THERE, LUTHOR.
I KNOW. I'VE KILLED BIG-SHOTS BEFORE.
NONSENSE.
THEY'LL SIMPLY CHOOSE ANOTHER AS THEIR FIGUREHEAD, AND HE'LL BE REDUCED TO NOTHING MORE THAN A CHEAP TABLOID CONSPIRACY FOR THE SUPERMARKET CLASSES.
BESIDES, THE TEMPORARY GRIEF OF THE NATION IS OF NO CONSEQUENCE WHEN YOU OPERATE AT MY LEVEL.
THIS MURDER IS MERELY A TACTICAL BUSINESS DECISION...
Shhh! YOU HEAR THAT WHISTLING SOUND OUTSIDE?
WALLS HAVE EARS IN THIS CITY, LUTHOR, OLD PAL.
LEXCORP
CLOSE ONE.

LARRY LIEBOWSKI, INDUSTRIAL ASSASSIN ALSO KNOWN AS MULTI-FACE, ALSO KNOWN AS ANYONE HE WANTS TO DISGUISE HIMSELF AS.
DESCRIBING HIM AS THE MAN OF A THOUSAND FACES DOESN'T BEGIN TO DO THIS GUY JUSTICE, SUPERMAN.
MULTI-FACE CAN ASSUME THE VOICE, POSTURE AND CREATE THE FEATURES OF ANYONE HE DESIRES. HE ALSO HAS THE ABILITY TO FOOL EVEN THE MOST SOPHISTICATED X-RAYS.
FBI SOURCES RECKON MULTI-FACE HAS BEEN HIRED TO CARRY OUT THE BIGGEST HIT OF HIS CAREER. THE BAD NEWS IS THAT HE'S NEVER MISSED A TARGET YET.
KLIK!
ANY QUESTIONS?
ONLY ONE, GENERAL HARDCASTLE.
WHY DON'T YOU LIKE HAVING ME AROUND THE WHITE HOUSE?

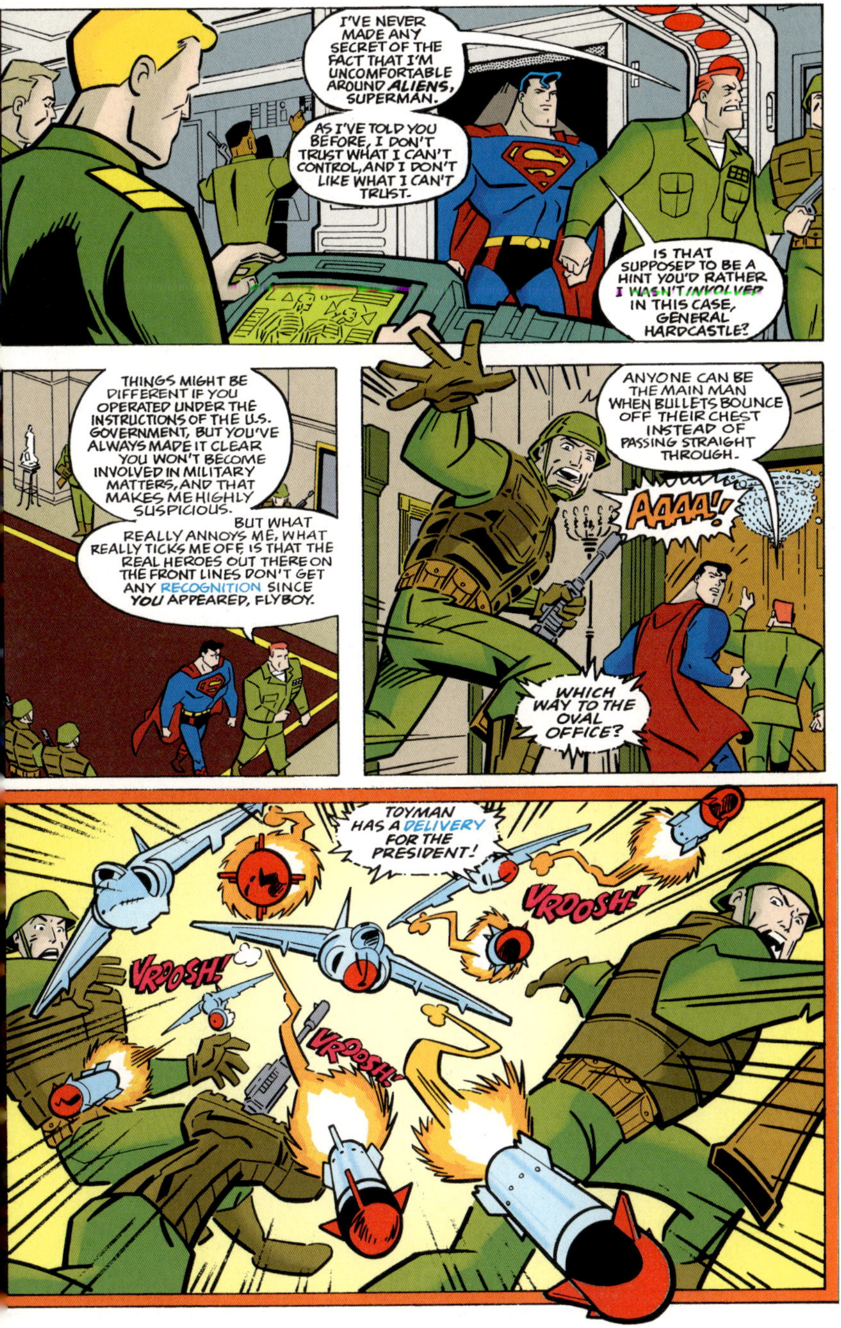
I'VE NEVER MADE ANY SECRET OF THE FACT THAT I'M UNCOMFORTABLE AROUND ALIENS, SUPERMAN.
AS I'VE TOLD YOU BEFORE, I DON'T TRUST WHAT I CAN'T CONTROL, AND I DON'T LIKE WHAT I CAN'T TRUST.
IS THAT SUPPOSED TO BE A HINT YOU'D RATHER I WASN'T INVOLVED IN THIS CASE, GENERAL HARDCASTLE?
THINGS MIGHT BE DIFFERENT IF YOU OPERATED UNDER THE INSTRUCTIONS OF THE U.S. GOVERNMENT, BUT YOU'VE ALWAYS MADE IT CLEAR YOU WON'T BECOME INVOLVED IN MILITARY MATTERS, AND THAT MAKES ME HIGHLY SUSPICIOUS.
BUT WHAT REALLY ANNOYS ME, WHAT REALLY TICKS ME OFF, IS THAT THE REAL HEROES OUT THERE ON THE FRONT LINES DON'T GET ANY RECOGNITION SINCE YOU APPEARED, FLYBOY.
ANYONE CAN BE THE MAIN MAN WHEN BULLETS BOUNCE OFF THEIR CHEST INSTEAD OF PASSING STRAIGHT THROUGH.
AAAA!
WHICH WAY TO THE OVAL OFFICE?
TOYMAN HAS A DELIVERY FOR THE PRESIDENT!
VROOSH!
VROOSH!
VROOSH!

TOYMAN, YOU MANIAC!
WHAT DO YOU THINK YOU'RE DOING?!
SKRUNCH!
BOOM!
BABOOM!
KABOOM!
TRYING TO EARN A BILLION DOLLARS BY REMOTE CONTROL FROM A SECRET LOCATION, SUPERMAN. WHAT DO YOU THINK?
BY THE WAY, THIS CHILDHOOD FAVORITE IS CARRYING A HIROSHIMA SPECIAL SET TO DETONATE IN TEN SECONDS...
...FOUR OF WHICH HAVE ALREADY PASSED.
WHAT DID HE SAY, SUPERMAN?

FIVE...
...FOUR...
...THREE...
...TWO...
...ONE...

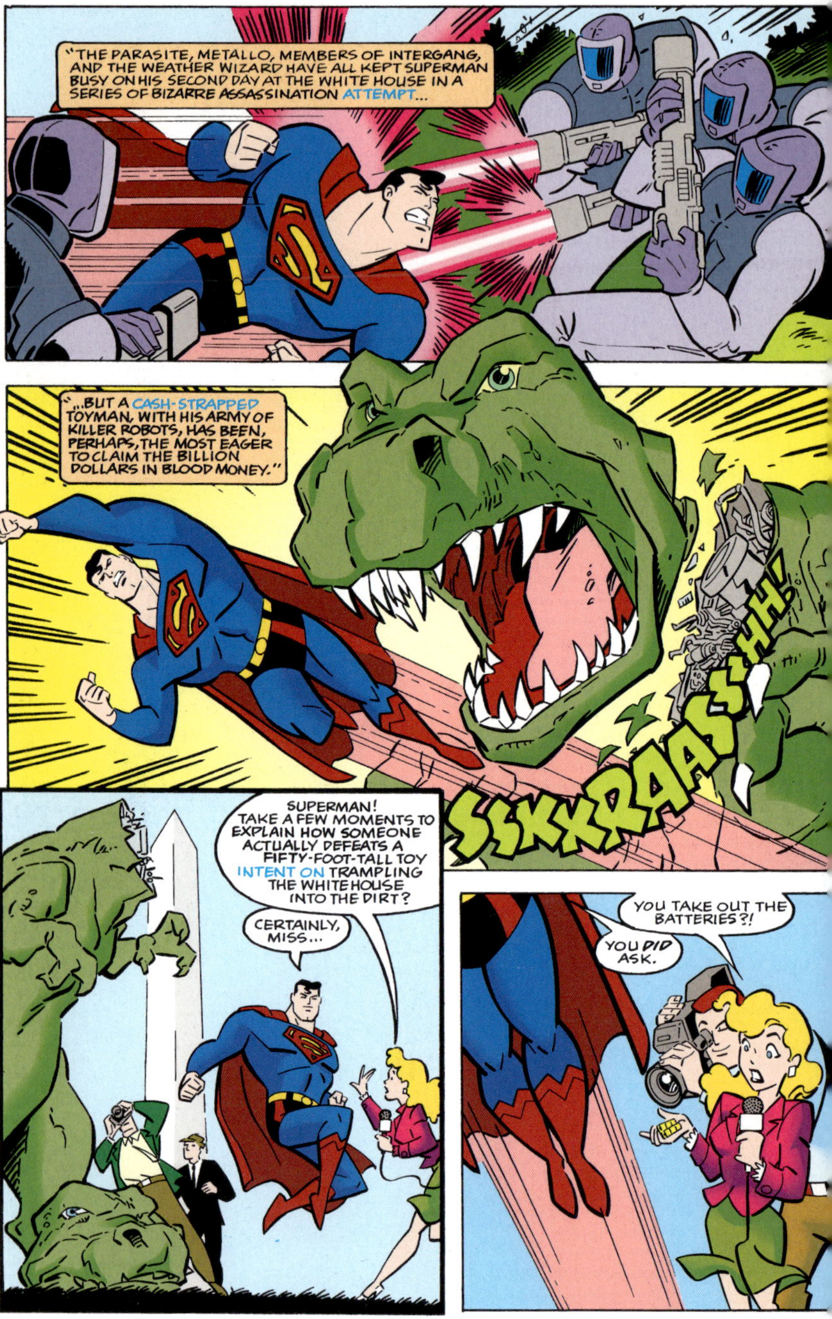
"THE PARASITE, METALLO, MEMBERS OF INTERGANG, AND THE WEATHER WIZARD HAVE ALL KEPT SUPERMAN BUSY ON HIS SECOND DAY AT THE WHITE HOUSE IN A SERIES OF BIZARRE ASSASSINATION ATTEMPT...
"...BUT A CASH-STRAPPED TOYMAN, WITH HIS ARMY OF KILLER ROBOTS, HAS BEEN, PERHAPS, THE MOST EAGER TO CLAIM THE BILLION DOLLARS IN BLOOD MONEY."
SSKKRAASSHH!
SUPERMAN! TAKE A FEW MOMENTS TO EXPLAIN HOW SOMEONE ACTUALLY DEFEATS A FIFTY-FOOT-TALL TOY INTENT ON TRAMPLING THE WHITE HOUSE INTO THE DIRT?
CERTAINLY, MISS...
YOU TAKE OUT THE BATTERIES?!
YOU DID ASK.

CONTROL, WE'VE GOT A MISS LANE HERE FROM THE DAILY PLANET SEEKING ACCESS TO THE PRESS SECTION. I CAN'T FIND HER NAME ON ANY OF THE LISTS.
NO NAME MEANS NO AUTHORIZATION, SECURITY FOUR. WE CAN'T BEND THE RULES FOR ANYONE WHEN THE PRESIDENT IS THIS CLOSE TO SIGNING THE PEACE TREATY.
SORRY, MISS LANE. I'M AFRAID I'M GOING TO HAVE TO ASK YOU TO LEAVE THE PREMISES.
THIS IS INSANE! FIRST THE HOTEL IS STILL BOOKED IN CLARK KENT'S NAME, AND NOW I CAN'T EVEN GET INTO THE STUPID PRESS CONFERENCE!
ALLOW ME TO ESCORT YOU, LOIS. I ALWAYS BOOK AN EXTRA SEAT IN CASE I FIND A DAMSEL IN DISTRESS.
FRANKLY, I DIDN'T THINK A PEACE SUMMIT WAS A TYPICAL NIGHT OUT FOR A NOTORIOUS WEAPONS MANUFACTURER LIKE YOU, LEX LUTHOR.
AS EVER, MY DEAR, YOU COMPLETELY MISJUDGE ME.
I WOULDN'T MISS THIS FOR THE WORLD.

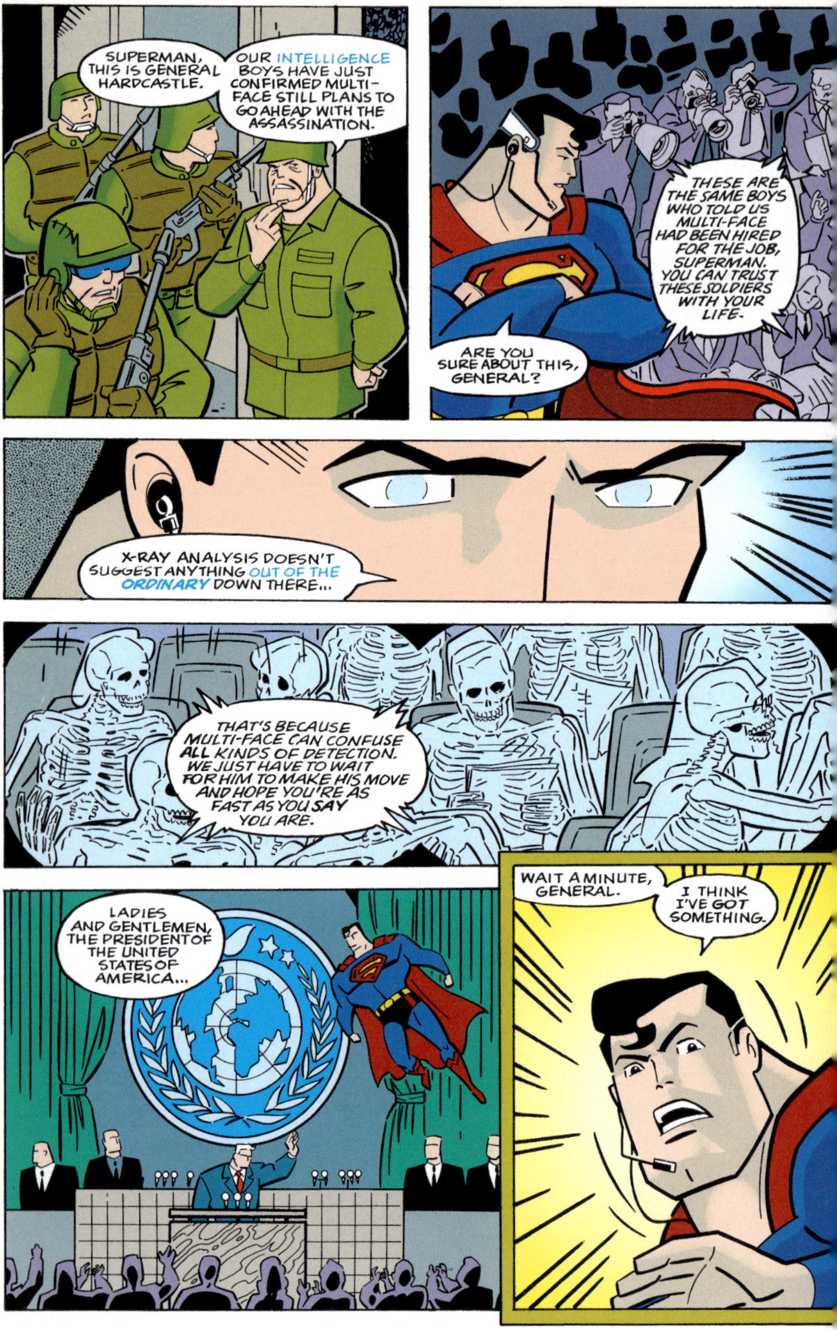
SUPERMAN, THIS IS GENERAL HARDCASTLE.
OUR INTELLIGENCE BOYS HAVE JUST CONFIRMED MULTI-FACE STILL PLANS TO GO AHEAD WITH THE ASSASSINATION.
THESE ARE THE SAME BOYS WHO TOLD US MULTI-FACE HAD BEEN HIRED FOR THE JOB, SUPERMAN. YOU CAN TRUST THESE SOLDIERS WITH YOUR LIFE.
ARE YOU SURE ABOUT THIS, GENERAL?
X-RAY ANALYSIS DOESN'T SUGGEST ANYTHING OUT OF THE ORDINARY DOWN THERE...
THAT'S BECAUSE MULTI-FACE CAN CONFUSE ALL KINDS OF DETECTION. WE JUST HAVE TO WAIT FOR HIM TO MAKE HIS MOVE AND HOPE YOU'RE AS FAST AS YOU SAY YOU ARE.
LADIES AND GENTLEMEN, THE PRESIDENT OF THE UNITED STATES OF AMERICA...
WAIT A MINUTE, GENERAL.
I THINK I'VE GOT SOMETHING.

I DON'T BELIEVE THIS.
WHAT IS IT, SUPERMAN? WHAT'S WRONG?
TALK ABOUT THE WRONG FACE AT THE WRONG TIME.
WOULD THE GENTLEMAN DISGUISED AS THE DAILY PLANET REPORTER IN THE THIRD ROW PLEASE STAND UP AND REMOVE HIS MASK?
HOW IN THE NAME OF...?
WHAT IS IT, SOLDIER? SUPERMAN'S JUST CAUGHT MULTI-FACE OUT THERE!
GENERAL, I THINK THERE'S SOMETHING YOU SHOULD KNOW...

YOU IDIOTIC LUNK!
DO YOU REALLY THINK THIS INTERVENTION IS GOING TO DIVERT ME FROM MY MISSION FOR A SECOND?
READ THE PAPERS, MULTI-FACE. BULLETS TEND TO BOUNCE OFF MY CHEST, BUT YOU'RE WELCOME TO TRY.
SUPERMAN, GET OUT OF THE WAY!
YOU'RE THE ONE HE WAS HIRED TO KILL!
SHUT UP!
CHOOOOM!

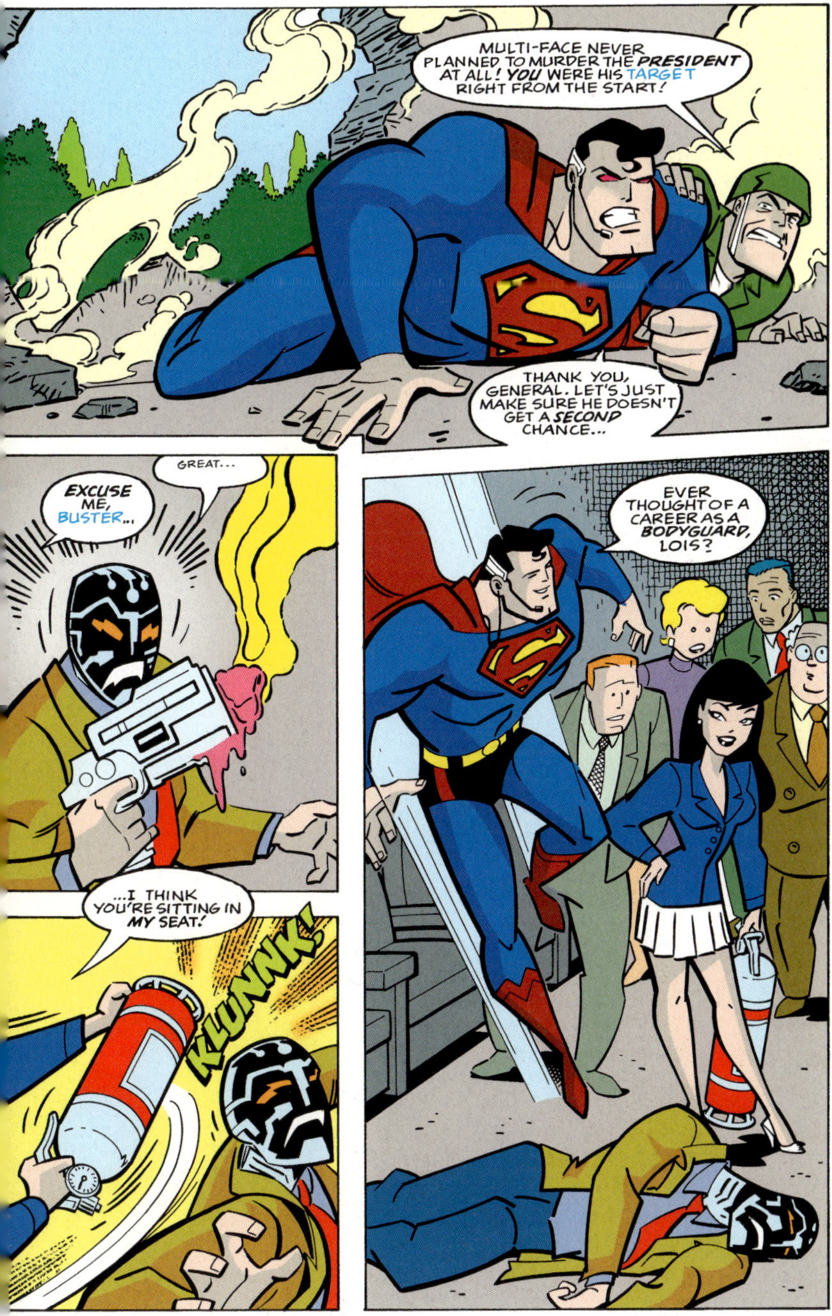
MULTI-FACE NEVER PLANNED TO MURDER THE PRESIDENT AT ALL! YOU WERE HIS TARGET RIGHT FROM THE START!
THANK YOU, GENERAL. LET'S JUST MAKE SURE HE DOESN'T GET A SECOND CHANCE...
EXCUSE ME, BUSTER...
GREAT...
...I THINK YOU'RE SITTING IN MY SEAT!
KLUNNK!
EVER THOUGHT OF A CAREER AS A BODYGUARD, LOIS?

DAILY PLANET
SECURITY SERVICE FOILS PLOT TO KILL SUPERMAN
EXCLUSIVE BY LOIS LANE
TYPICAL OF SUPERMAN TO BE SO CONCERNED ABOUT SOMEONE ELSE. HE DIDN'T REALIZE HE WAS THE ONE MULTI-FACE WAS AIMING FOR WITH THAT HIGH-IMPACT BLASTER.
AND TO THINK THE SCOOP COULD HAVE BEEN YOURS IF YOU HADN'T OPTED FOR THE SQUARE DANCE, KENT.
ALL'S FAIR IN LOVE AND PRINT JOURNALISM, LOIS.
DAILY PLANET
SECURITY SERVICES FOILS PLOT TO K
SUPERM
KENT, STOP TALKING AND START TYPING! TWO DAYS' VACATION MEANS YOU HAVE TO WORK TWICE AS HARD WHEN YOU GET BACK, AND I DON'T WANT TO HEAR ANY EXCUSES!
WOW. WELCOME BACK, huh?
WAIT A MINUTE! THIS DOESN'T MAKE ANY SENSE...
IF MULTI-FACE WAS HIRED AS AN ASSASSIN, WHY DID HE AIM FOR SUPERMAN WHEN HE COULD HAVE TAKEN A SHOT AT THE PRESIDENT AND EARNED HIMSELF A BILLION DOLLARS?!
I DIDN'T KNOW HE WAS THAT PATRIOTIC.
UNFORTUNATELY, HE'S NOT, JIMMY. WORD IS HE WAS OFFERED TWO BILLION DOLLARS TO GET RID OF SUPERMAN.
I JUST HOPE THE PRESIDENT DOESN'T TAKE IT PERSONALLY.
THE End

WAR GAMES
PART 1
"WHAT DO YOU FIGURE'S CAUSING ALL THE EXCITEMENT, Mr. KENT? NOT MORE COMPUTER TROUBLE..."
MARK MILLAR - WRITER
ALUIR AMANCIO - PENCILLER
TERRY AUSTIN - INKER
MARIE SEVERIN - COLORIST
LOIS BUHALIS - LETTERER
FRANK BERRIOS - ASSISTANT EDITOR
MIKE McAVENNIE - EDITOR
SUPERMAN CREATED BY JERRY SIEGEL & JOE SHUSTER

Mr. KENT? WHERE--?
HOW DOES HE DO THAT?
EVERYBODY OFF THE BRIDGE!
IT'S NO USE! WE CAN'T STEER THE SHIP CLEAR IN TIME!
B-BUT THE COAST GUARD SAID THE BRIDGE WAS RAISED!
WELL, THEY WERE WRONG, AND THOSE POOR DEVILS DON'T STAND A CHANCE! GET INTO CRASH POSITION!
WE'RE DEAD, WE'RE... HUH?
MAN, WOULD YOU LOOK AT THAT!
THIS IS WHY WE NEVER MOVED TO GOTHAM CITY.
AWESOME, DUDE, TOTALLY AWESOME.

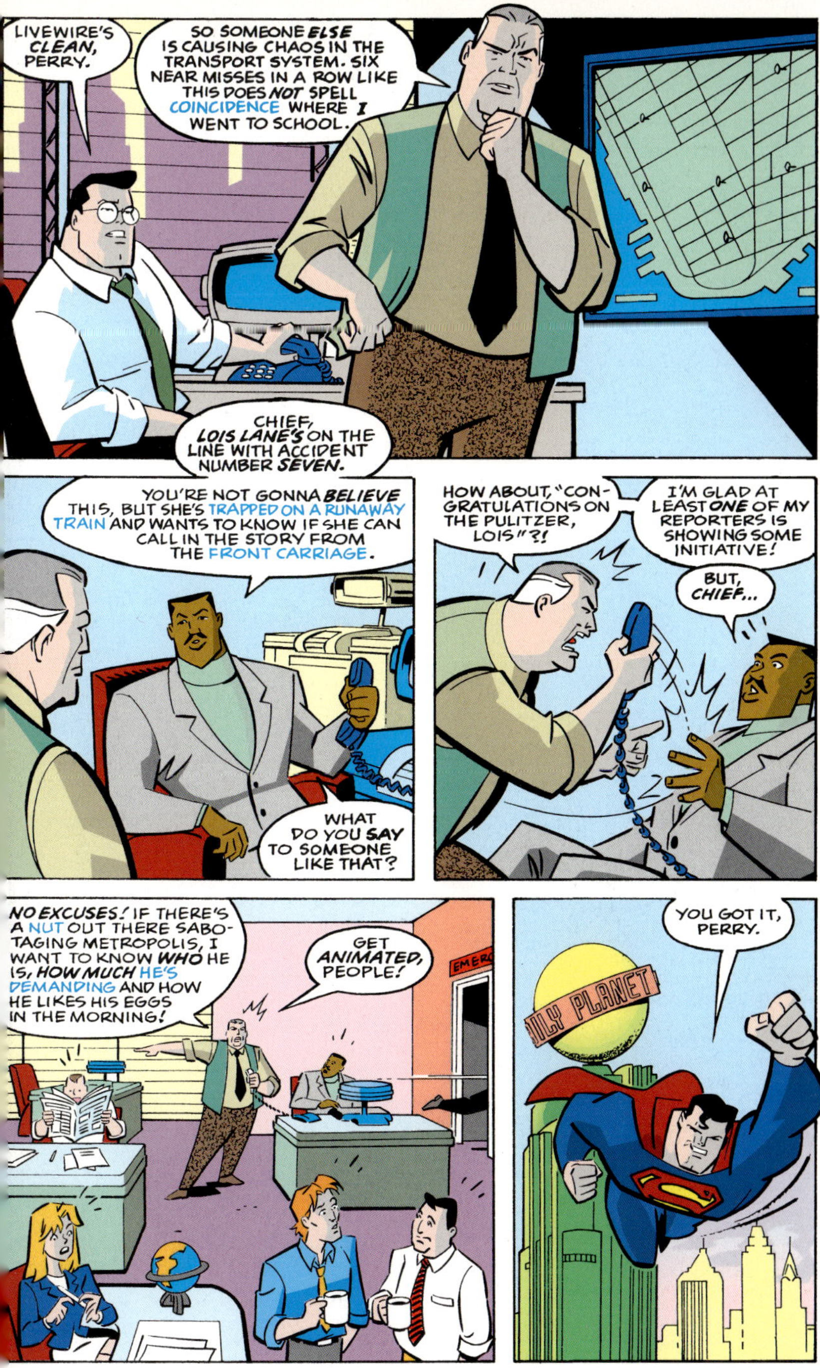
LIVEWIRE'S CLEAN, PERRY.
SO SOMEONE ELSE IS CAUSING CHAOS IN THE TRANSPORT SYSTEM. SIX NEAR MISSES IN A ROW LIKE THIS DOES NOT SPELL COINCIDENCE WHERE I WENT TO SCHOOL.
CHIEF, LOIS LANE'S ON THE LINE WITH ACCIDENT NUMBER SEVEN.
YOU'RE NOT GONNA BELIEVE THIS, BUT SHE'S TRAPPED ON A RUNAWAY TRAIN AND WANTS TO KNOW IF SHE CAN CALL IN THE STORY FROM THE FRONT CARRIAGE.
WHAT DO YOU SAY TO SOMEONE LIKE THAT?
HOW ABOUT, "CONGRATULATIONS ON THE PULITZER, LOIS"?!
I'M GLAD AT LEAST ONE OF MY REPORTERS IS SHOWING SOME INITIATIVE!
BUT, CHIEF...
NO EXCUSES! IF THERE'S A NUT OUT THERE SABOTAGING METROPOLIS, I WANT TO KNOW WHO HE IS, HOW MUCH HE'S DEMANDING AND HOW HE LIKES HIS EGGS IN THE MORNING!
GET ANIMATED, PEOPLE!
YOU GOT IT, PERRY.

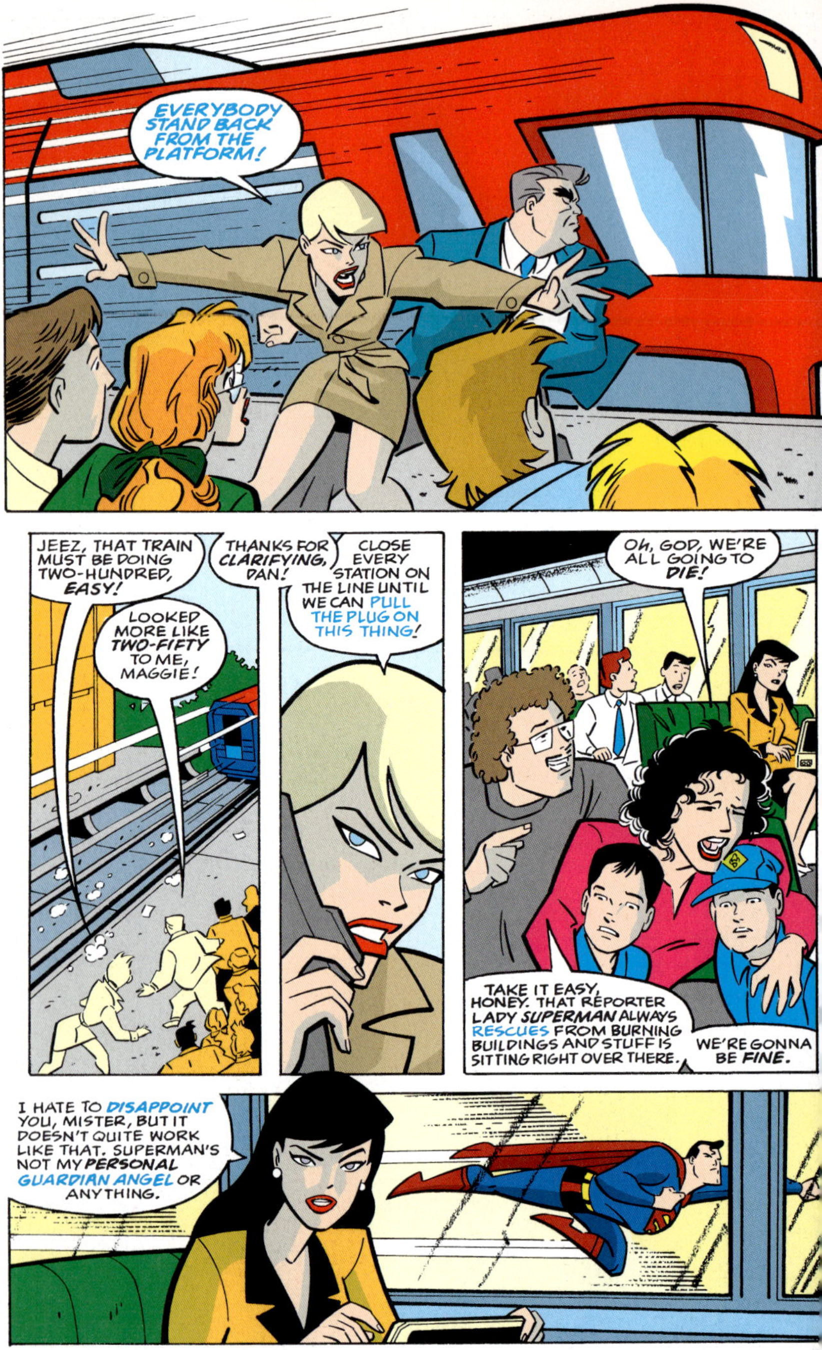
EVERYBODY STAND BACK FROM THE PLATFORM!
JEEZ, THAT TRAIN MUST BE DOING TWO-HUNDRED, EASY!
LOOKED MORE LIKE TWO-FIFTY TO ME, MAGGIE!
THANKS FOR CLARIFYING, DAN!
CLOSE EVERY STATION ON THE LINE UNTIL WE CAN PULL THE PLUG ON THIS THING!
OH, GOD, WE'RE ALL GOING TO DIE!
TAKE IT EASY, HONEY. THAT REPORTER LADY SUPERMAN ALWAYS RESCUES FROM BURNING BUILDINGS AND STUFF IS SITTING RIGHT OVER THERE.
WE'RE GONNA BE FINE.
I HATE TO DISAPPOINT YOU, MISTER, BUT IT DOESN'T QUITE WORK LIKE THAT. SUPERMAN'S NOT MY PERSONAL GUARDIAN ANGEL OR ANYTHING.

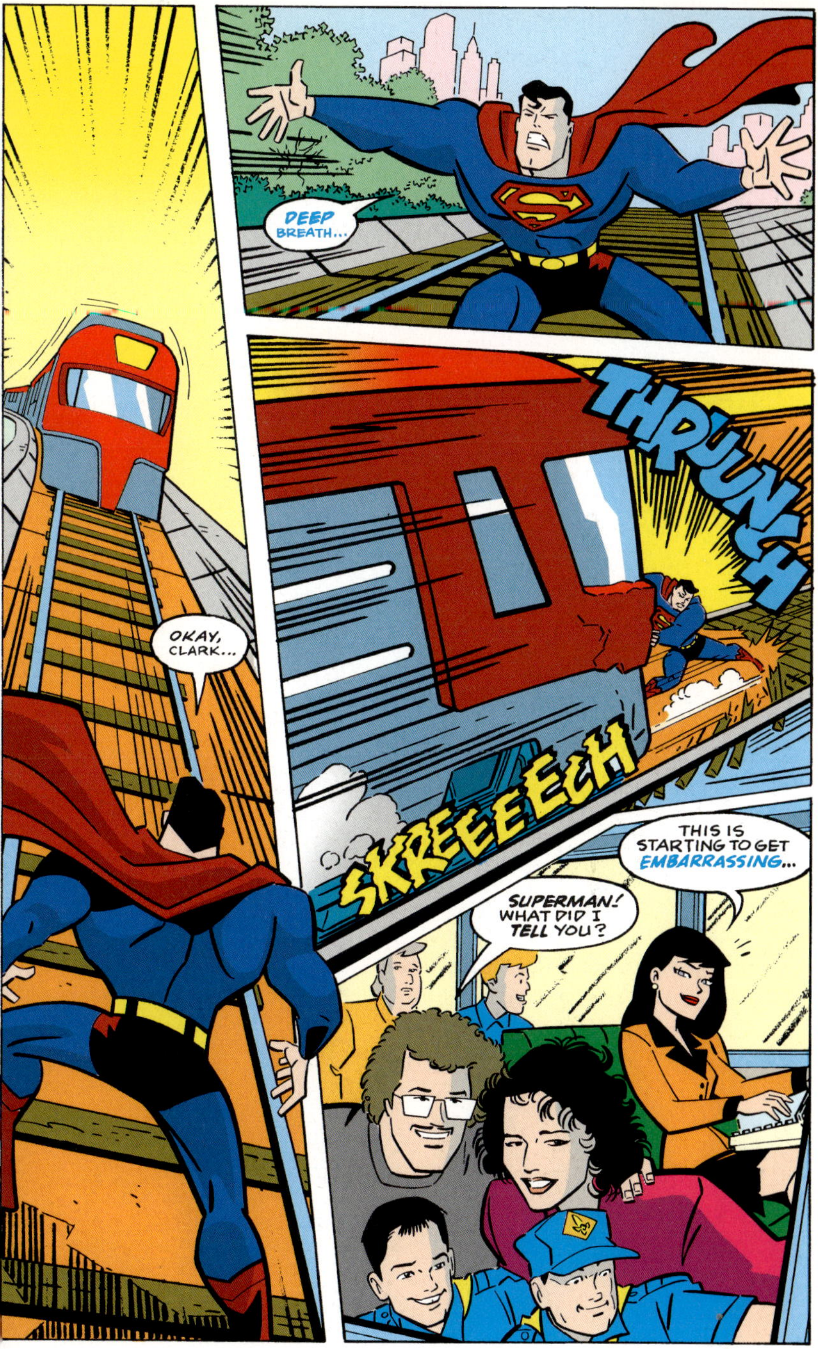
DEEP BREATH...
OKAY, CLARK...
THRUNCH
SKREEEEECH
THIS IS STARTING TO GET EMBARRASSING...
SUPERMAN! WHAT DID I TELL YOU?

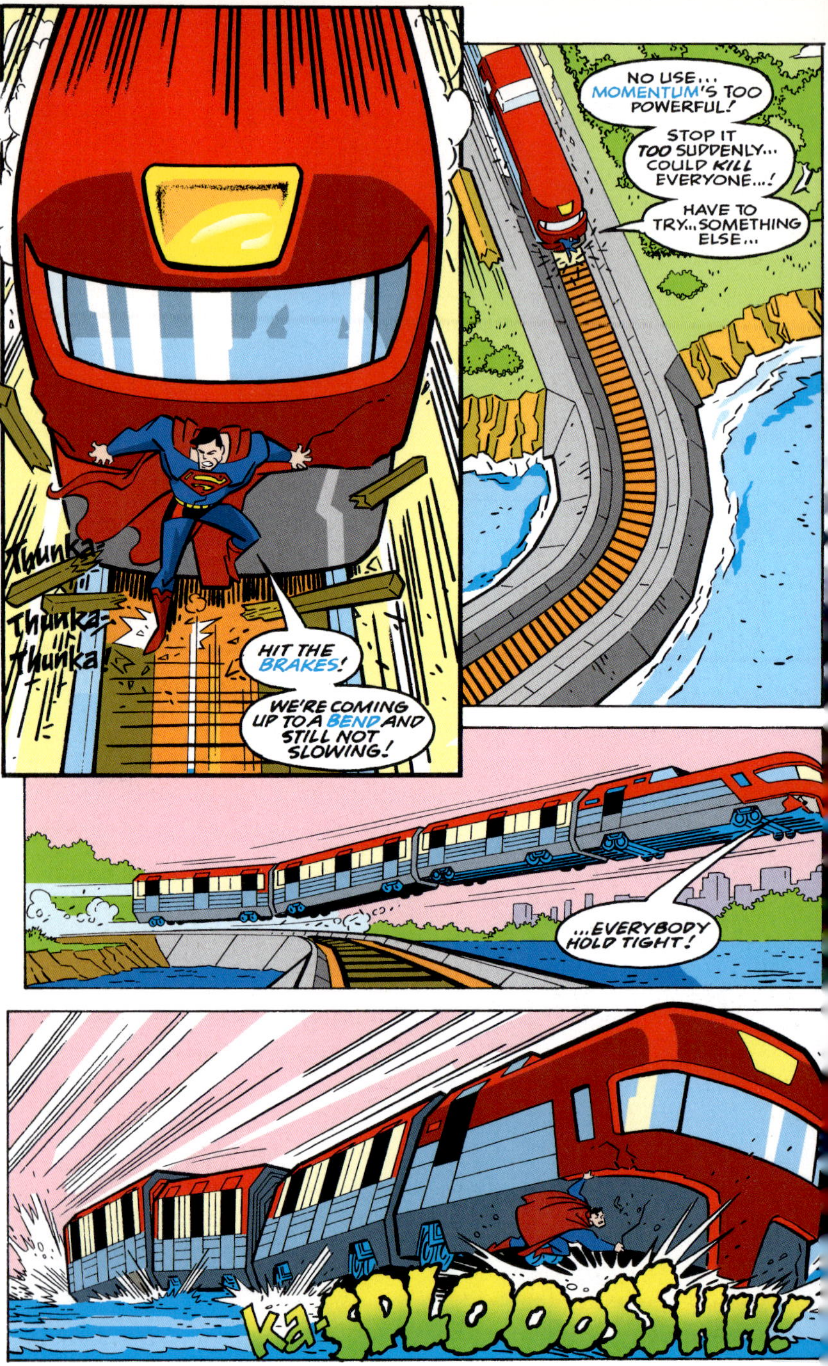
Thunka-
Thunka-
Thunka!
HIT THE BRAKES!
WE'RE COMING UP TO A BEND AND STILL NOT SLOWING!
NO USE... MOMENTUM'S TOO POWERFUL!
STOP IT TOO SUDDENLY... COULD KILL EVERYONE...!
HAVE TO TRY... SOMETHING ELSE...
...EVERYBODY HOLD TIGHT!
KA-SPLOOOoSSHH!

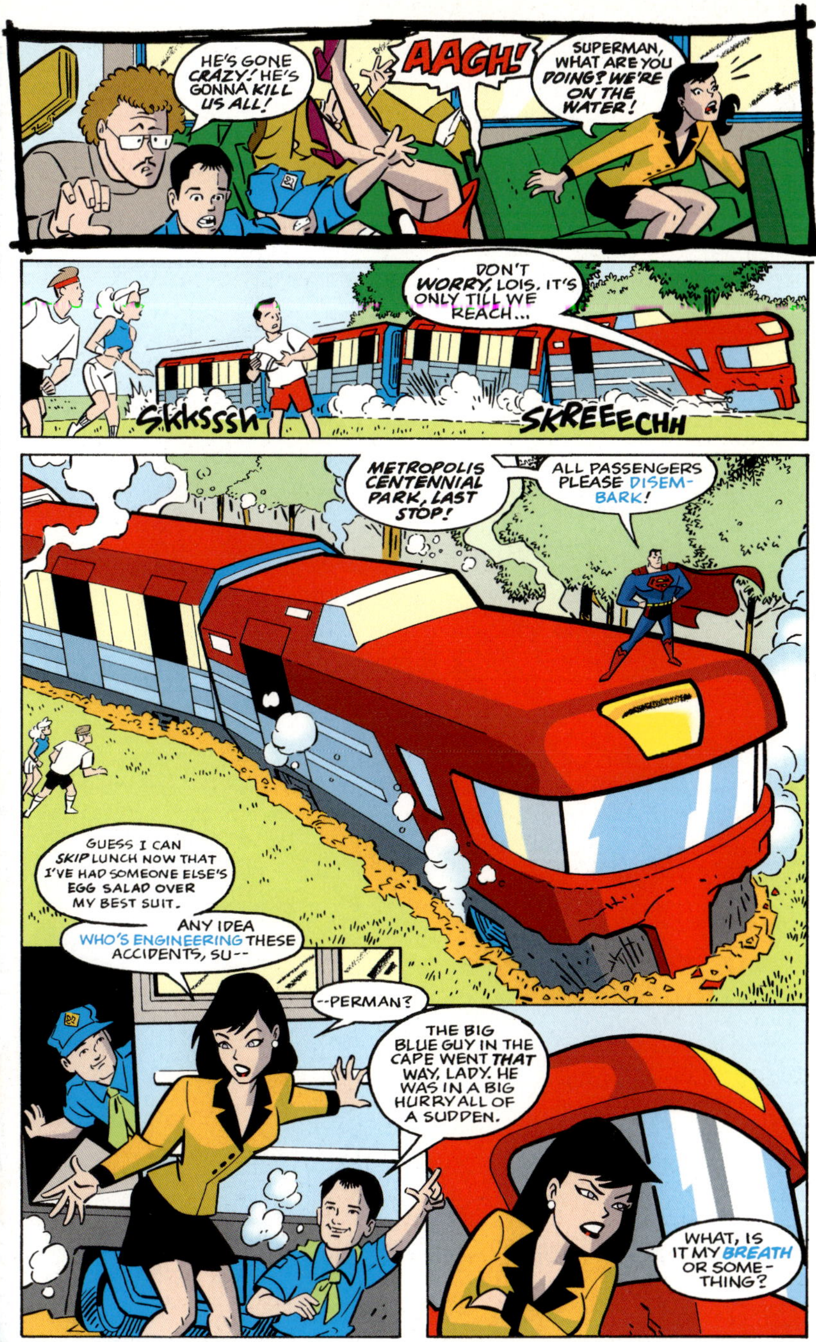
HE'S GONE CRAZY! HE'S GONNA KILL US ALL!
AAGH!
SUPERMAN, WHAT ARE YOU DOING? WE'RE ON THE WATER!
DON'T WORRY, LOIS. IT'S ONLY TILL WE REACH...
SKKSSSH
SKREEECHH
METROPOLIS CENTENNIAL PARK, LAST STOP!
ALL PASSENGERS PLEASE DISEMBARK!
GUESS I CAN SKIP LUNCH NOW THAT I'VE HAD SOMEONE ELSE'S EGG SALAD OVER MY BEST SUIT.
ANY IDEA WHO'S ENGINEERING THESE ACCIDENTS, SU--
--PERMAN?
THE BIG BLUE GUY IN THE CAPE WENT THAT WAY, LADY. HE WAS IN A BIG HURRY ALL OF A SUDDEN.
WHAT, IS IT MY BREATH OR SOMETHING?

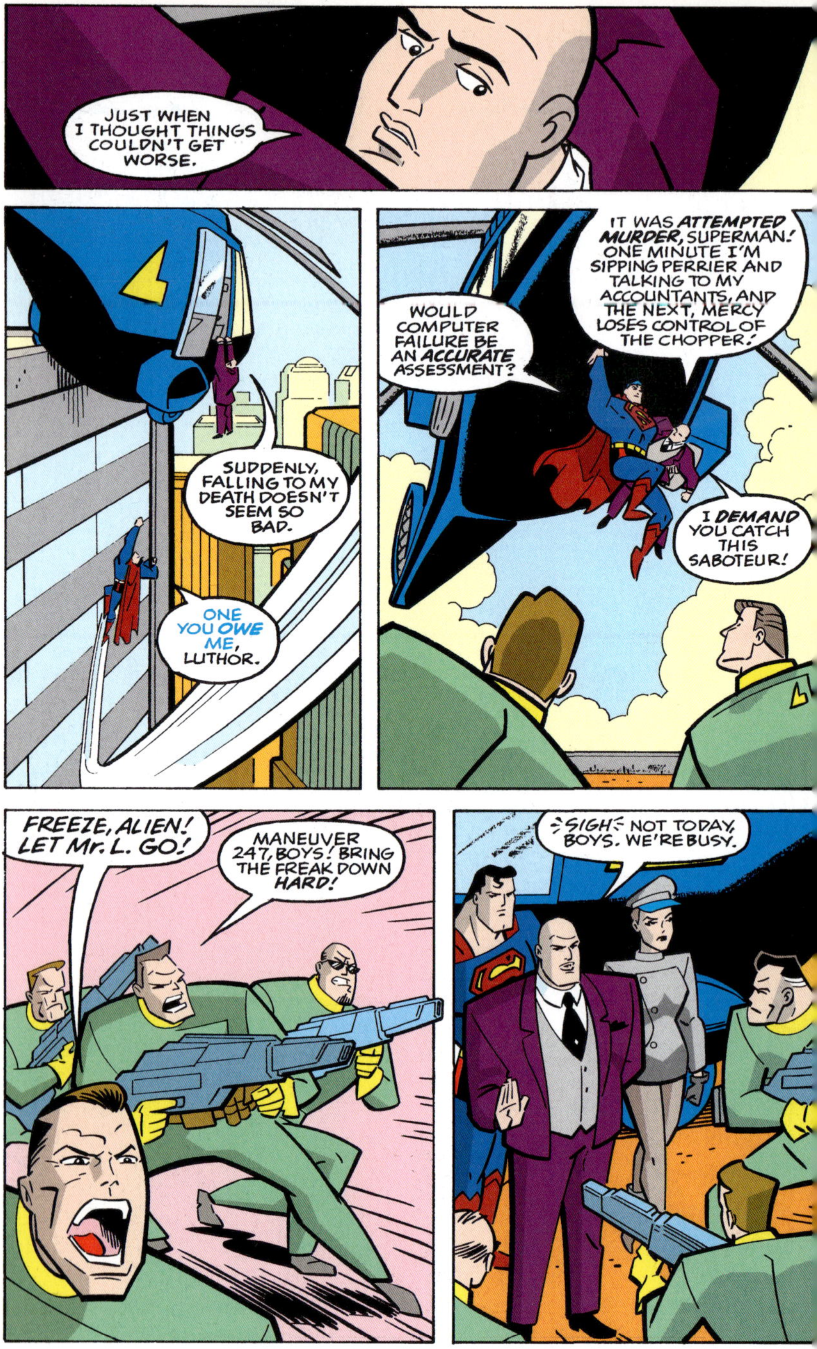
JUST WHEN I THOUGHT THINGS COULDN'T GET WORSE.
SUDDENLY, FALLING TO MY DEATH DOESN'T SEEM SO BAD.
ONE YOU OWE ME, LUTHOR.
IT WAS ATTEMPTED MURDER, SUPERMAN! ONE MINUTE I'M SIPPING PERRIER AND TALKING TO MY ACCOUNTANTS, AND THE NEXT, MERCY LOSES CONTROL OF THE CHOPPER!
WOULD COMPUTER FAILURE BE AN ACCURATE ASSESSMENT?
I DEMAND YOU CATCH THIS SABOTEUR!
FREEZE, ALIEN! LET Mr. L. GO!
MANEUVER 247, BOYS! BRING THE FREAK DOWN HARD!
SIGH NOT TODAY, BOYS. WE'RE BUSY.

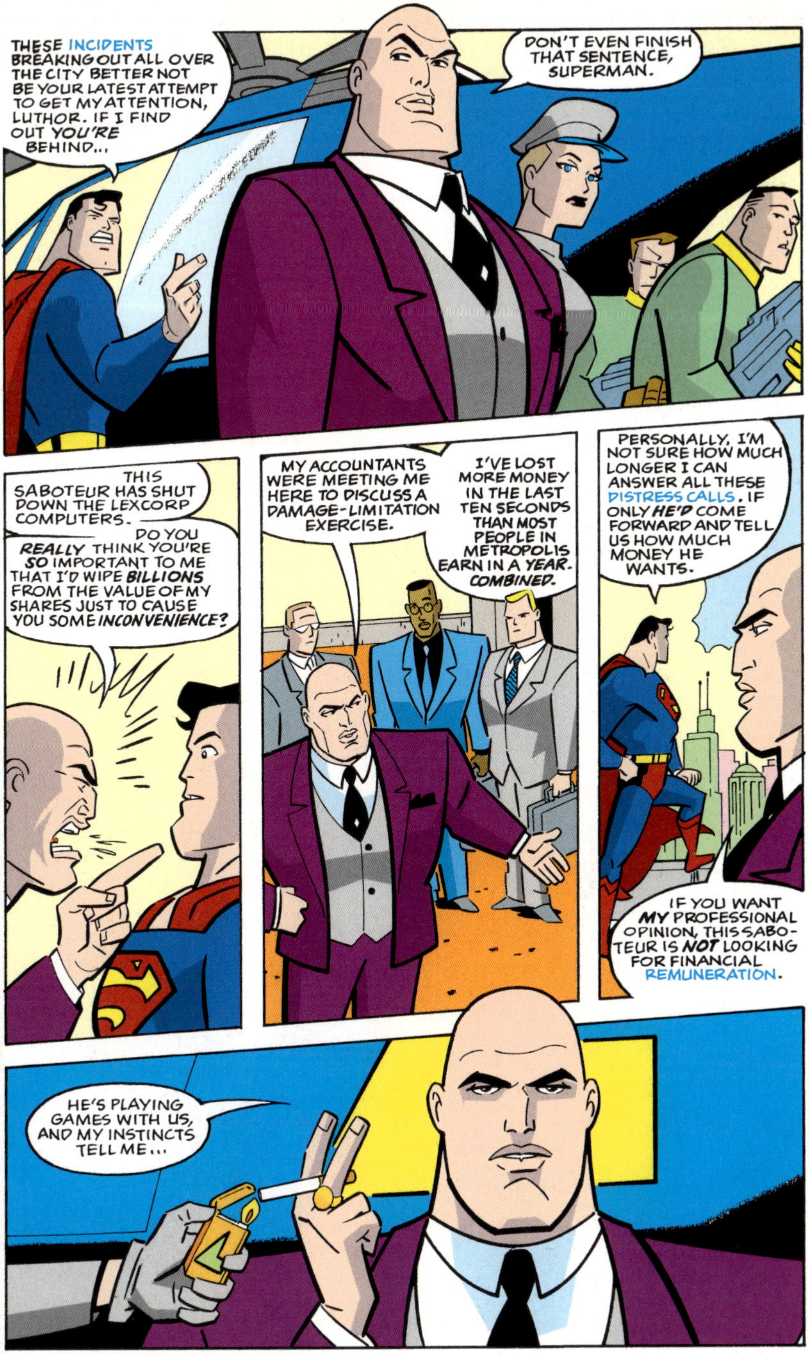
THESE INCIDENTS BREAKING OUT ALL OVER THE CITY BETTER NOT BE YOUR LATEST ATTEMPT TO GET MY ATTENTION, LUTHOR. IF I FIND OUT YOU'RE BEHIND...
DON'T EVEN FINISH THAT SENTENCE, SUPERMAN.
THIS SABOTEUR HAS SHUT DOWN THE LEXCORP COMPUTERS.
DO YOU REALLY THINK YOU'RE SO IMPORTANT TO ME THAT I'D WIPE BILLIONS FROM THE VALUE OF MY SHARES JUST TO CAUSE YOU SOME INCONVENIENCE?
MY ACCOUNTANTS WERE MEETING ME HERE TO DISCUSS A DAMAGE-LIMITATION EXERCISE.
I'VE LOST MORE MONEY IN THE LAST TEN SECONDS THAN MOST PEOPLE IN METROPOLIS EARN IN A YEAR. COMBINED.
PERSONALLY, I'M NOT SURE HOW MUCH LONGER I CAN ANSWER ALL THESE DISTRESS CALLS. IF ONLY HE'D COME FORWARD AND TELL US HOW MUCH MONEY HE WANTS.
IF YOU WANT MY PROFESSIONAL OPINION, THIS SABOTEUR IS NOT LOOKING FOR FINANCIAL REMUNERATION.
HE'S PLAYING GAMES WITH US, AND MY INSTINCTS TELL ME...

"...THINGS ARE ABOUT TO GET SERIOUS."
SORRY, SUPERMAN...
BERRIOS
MCA
...IF ONLY YOU'D GOT HERE...
...A FEW MINUTES EARLIER...
PARAMEDICS

BASEMENT
UNFORTUNATELY, SUPERMAN WAS IN ORBIT, RESCUING THE STRANDED S.T.A.R. LABS SHUTTLE AS THE ELEVATOR PLUNGED THE FULL FIFTY-TWO STORIES AND...
KLIK!
I THINK WE GET THE PICTURE.
GEEZ, MISS LANE, THIS IS KINDA LIKE THE WAY THINGS WERE BEFORE SUPERMAN. YOU KNOW--PLANES JUST FALLING OUT OF THE SKY AND NO ONE TO CATCH THEM.
THE FRUSTRATION MUST BE KILLING HIM.
HOW CAN HE EVEN EXPECT TO KEEP UP THE PACE?
SUPERMAN CAN ONLY BE IN ONE PLACE AT A TIME, BUT WHOEVER'S INFILTRATED THE COMPUTER SYSTEM CAN MAKE A THOUSAND ACCIDENTS HAPPEN SIMULTANEOUSLY.
JUST FIND SUPERMAN SOMEONE TO HIT, JIMMY.
WELL, LET'S SEE WHAT SOME OF MY HACKER BUDDIES HAVE COME UP WITH...
HEY, I THINK I'VE GOT SOMETHING HERE, MISS LANE, BUT I'M STARTING TO WISH WE HADN'T. LOOK...
THAT... THAT'S IMPOSSIBLE!
THAT THING IS DESTROYED!
WAIT A SECOND, I'M LOSING THE PICTURE...

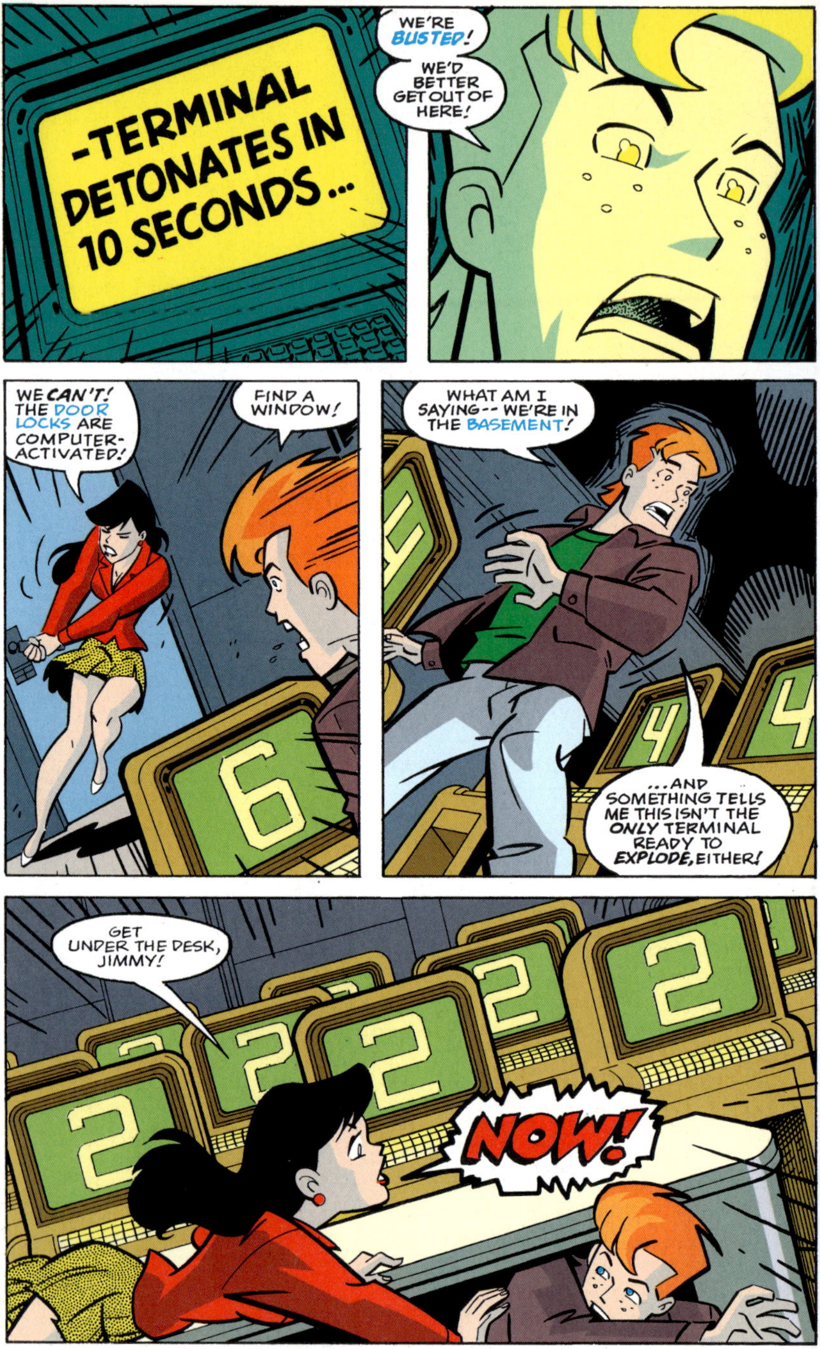
-TERMINAL DETONATES IN 10 SECONDS...
WE'RE BUSTED!
WE'D BETTER GET OUT OF HERE!
WE CAN'T! THE DOOR LOCKS ARE COMPUTER-ACTIVATED!
FIND A WINDOW!
6
WHAT AM I SAYING-- WE'RE IN THE BASEMENT!
...AND SOMETHING TELLS ME THIS ISN'T THE ONLY TERMINAL READY TO EXPLODE, EITHER!
GET UNDER THE DESK, JIMMY!
NOW!

BOOOM!
DID YOU HEAR THAT, PROFESSOR? FIRE ALARMS...
NO, BUT THEN, I DON'T HAVE YOUR HEARING, SUPERMAN.
THE EMERGENCY SERVICES IN METROPOLIS ARE QUITE COMPETENT, YOU KNOW. PLEASE TRY TO CONCENTRATE ON THE MAIN CRISIS HERE.
SORRY, PROFESSOR. IT'S JUST...
HOW MANY MORE EMERGENCIES CAN I RESPOND TO BEFORE EVEN I COLLAPSE FROM EXHAUSTION?
IF IT'S ANY CONSOLATION, WE'VE TRACED THE SOURCE OF THE PROBLEM.
ACCORDING TO THE COORDINATES, THE SABOTEUR IS BASED IN THE NORTH POLE, AND I THINK WE BOTH KNOW WHAT THAT MEANS...

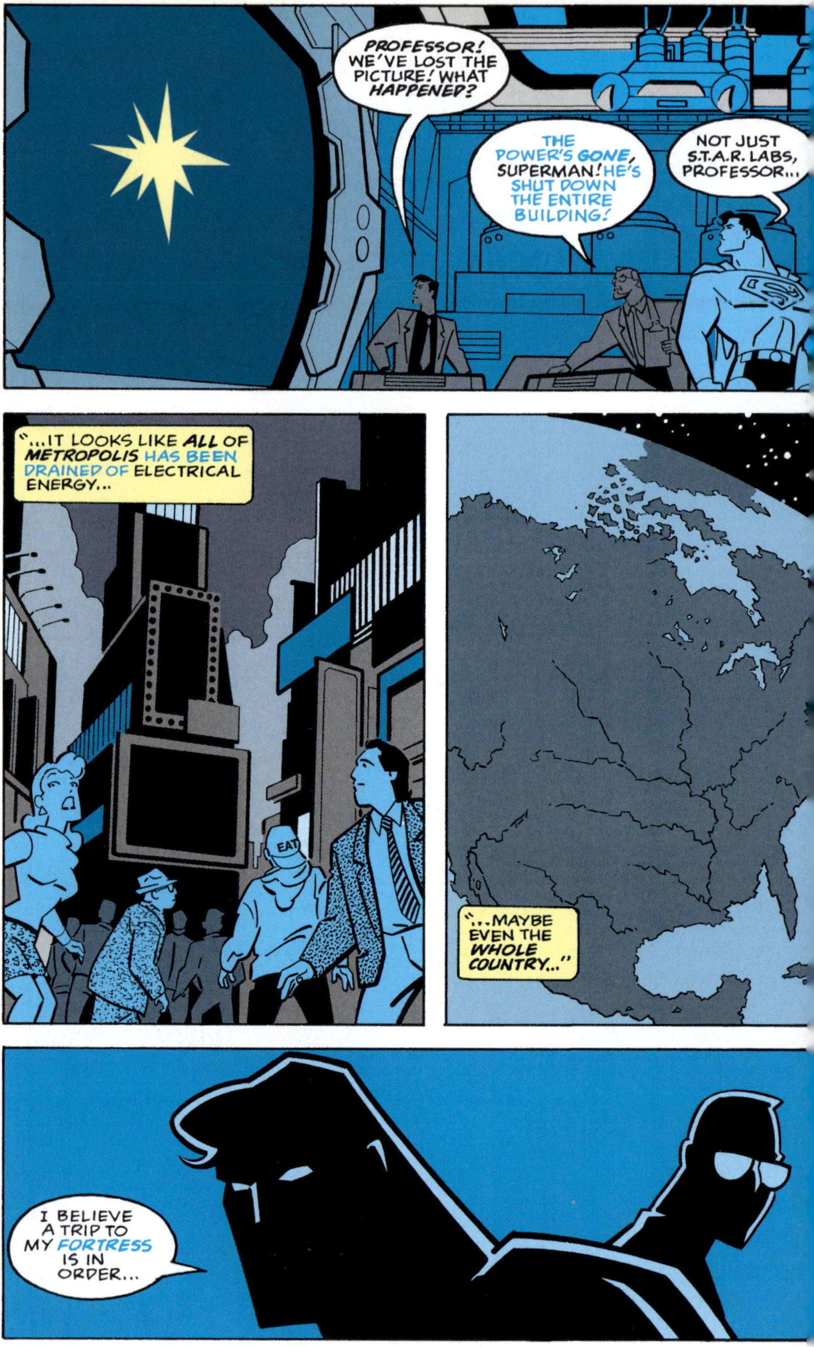
PROFESSOR! WE'VE LOST THE PICTURE! WHAT HAPPENED?
THE POWER'S GONE, SUPERMAN! HE'S SHUT DOWN THE ENTIRE BUILDING!
NOT JUST S.T.A.R. LABS, PROFESSOR...
"...IT LOOKS LIKE ALL OF METROPOLIS HAS BEEN DRAINED OF ELECTRICAL ENERGY...
EAT
"...MAYBE EVEN THE WHOLE COUNTRY..."
I BELIEVE A TRIP TO MY FORTRESS IS IN ORDER...

YOU REALLY DIDN'T HAVE TO DO THIS, PROFESSOR.
WHAT WAS THE ALTERNATIVE? SIT AT THE CANDLES AND PRAY WITH THE OTHERS?
"AT LEAST MY COMPUTER SKILLS MIGHT BE USEFUL WHEN WE ACTUALLY CONFRONT THIS THING."
THERE'S... THERE'S NO ONE HERE...
NOT SO, PROFESSOR. MY HEARING'S PICKING UP SOMEONE ELSE IN HERE...
...AND THE ORB CONTAINING KRYPTON'S ENTIRE HISTORY IS MISSING.
...WHICH CONFIRMS MY WORST FEARS.
SO... HOW DID YOU ESCAPE...

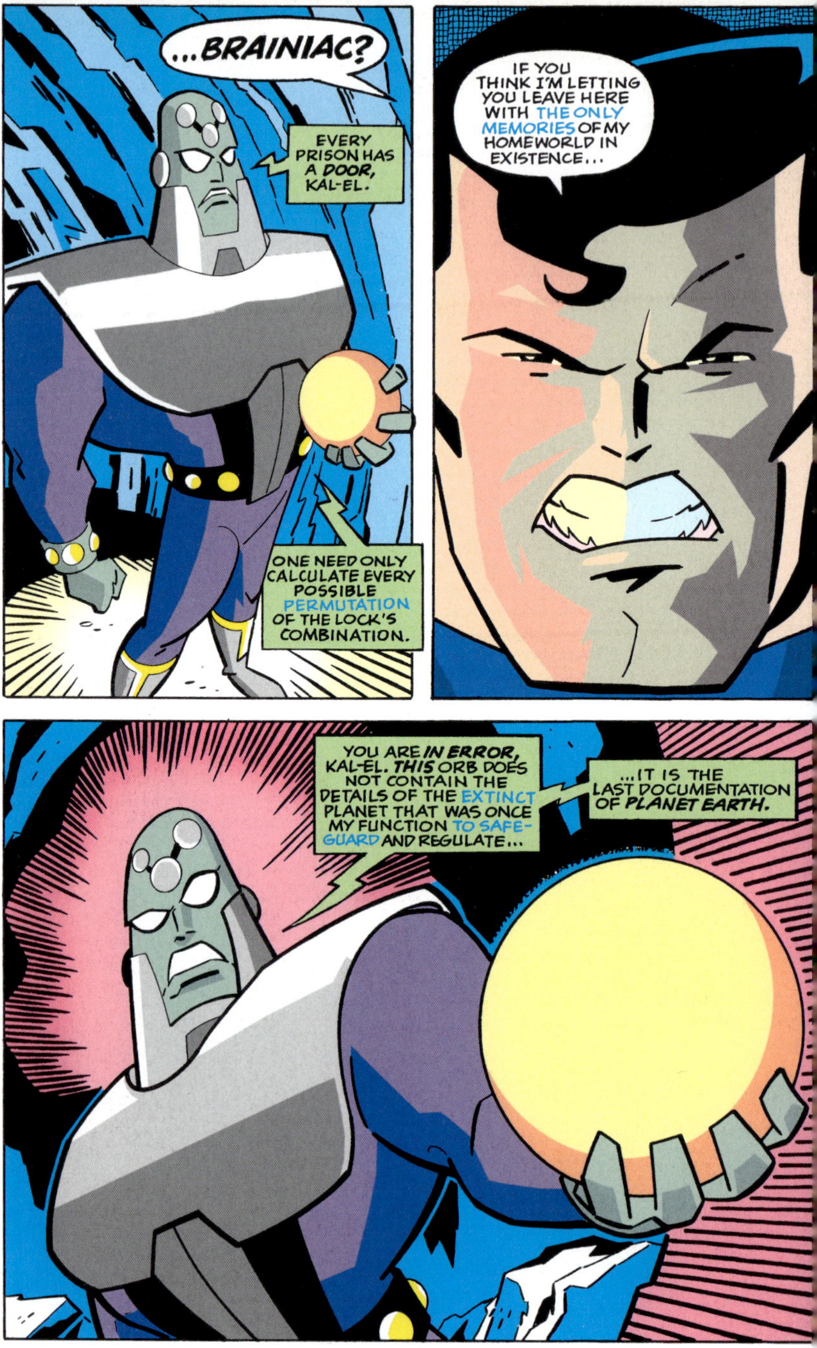
...BRAINIAC?
EVERY PRISON HAS A DOOR, KAL-EL.
ONE NEED ONLY CALCULATE EVERY POSSIBLE PERMUTATION OF THE LOCK'S COMBINATION.
IF YOU THINK I'M LETTING YOU LEAVE HERE WITH THE ONLY MEMORIES OF MY HOMEWORLD IN EXISTENCE...
YOU ARE IN ERROR, KAL-EL. THIS ORB DOES NOT CONTAIN THE DETAILS OF THE EXTINCT PLANET THAT WAS ONCE MY FUNCTION TO SAFE-GUARD AND REGULATE...
...IT IS THE LAST DOCUMENTATION OF PLANET EARTH.

ASSUMING CONTROL OF YOUR FORTRESS'S COMPUTER SYSTEM ALLOWED ME ACCESS TO ANY NETWORK I DESIRED, DISTRACTING BOTH YOU AND LUTHOR WHILE I REBUILT MY SHIP AND BODY IN SECLUSION...
...AT THE SAME TIME DOWN-LOADING DATA FROM EVERY COMPUTER FILE ON EARTH. THE INFORMATION HAS BEEN SECURED AND THUS THE ORIGINAL CAN BE DESTROYED.
EARTH HAS BECOME OBSOLETE.
WHAT DO YOU MEAN?
"I HAVE PRIMED EVERY NUCLEAR WARHEAD IN EXISTENCE FOR LAUNCH THIRTY MINUTES FROM NOW, LEAVING ME PRECISELY ENOUGH TIME TO VACATE THIS DOOMED WORLD.
"ITS PARALLELS WITH KRYPTON ARE FASCINATING..."
FORGET IT, BRAINIAC! YOU'RE GOING NOWHERE!
SHAZZAKK!

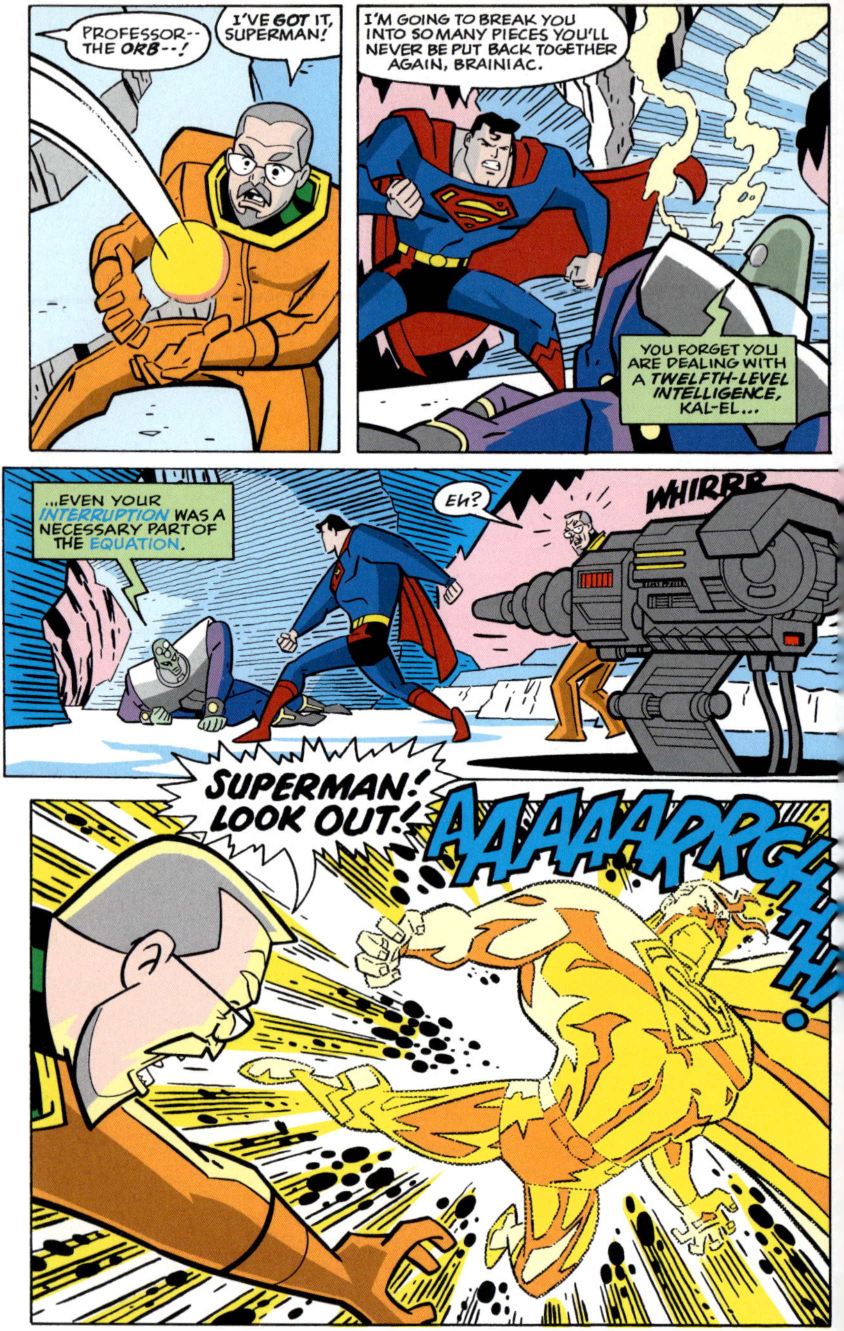
PROFESSOR-- THE ORB--!
I'VE GOT IT, SUPERMAN!
I'M GOING TO BREAK YOU INTO SO MANY PIECES YOU'LL NEVER BE PUT BACK TOGETHER AGAIN, BRAINIAC.
YOU FORGET YOU ARE DEALING WITH A TWELFTH-LEVEL INTELLIGENCE, KAL-EL...
...EVEN YOUR INTERRUPTION WAS A NECESSARY PART OF THE EQUATION.
Eh?
WHIRRR
SUPERMAN! LOOK OUT!
AAAAARRGHHH!

DEAR LORD...
A MAN OF SCIENCE USING A RELIGIOUS PHRASE IS MOST INTERESTING, PROFESSOR. HOWEVER, A RESPONSE IS NOT WHAT I REQUIRE FROM YOU.
THE EARTH ORB, PLEASE.
K-KEEP AWAY!
HIDING WILL ACHIEVE NOTHING, PROFESSOR. GIVE ME THE ORB NOW, OR YOUR DEATH WILL BE SLOW AND PAINFUL.
ONLY TWENTY-EIGHT MINUTES UNTIL ARMAGEDDON.
YOU'RE GOING TO KILL ME LIKE YOU KILLED SUPERMAN?
KAL-EL IS NOT DEAD, PROFESSOR. HIS INVULNERABILITY MEANT DESTROYING HIM REQUIRED TOO MUCH EFFORT.
I SIMPLY PLACED HIM IN THE LIMBO STATE INVENTED BY HIS FATHER TO IMPRISON KRYPTON'S UNDESIRABLES...

"...HE IS TRAPPED IN THE PHANTOM ZONE."

YOU MISUNDERSTAND THE SITUATION *ENTIRELY*, PROFESSOR.
STOPPING THE MISSILES NOW WOULD BE *IMPOSSIBLE* WITHOUT FUSING EVERY CIRCUIT IN MY SYSTEM.
EARTH DIES IN TWENTY-SIX MINUTES.
THE ONLY VARIABLE IS WHETHER YOU DELIVER THE ORB *VOLUNTARILY*, OR IF I MUST PRY IT FROM YOUR COLD, DEAD FINGERS...
SUPERMAN...!
YOU ARE WASTING YOUR FEW REMAINING BREATHS, PROFESSOR...
"...KAL-EL CAN HEAR NOTHING FROM THE *PHANTOM ZONE*."

THE BLACKOUT HAS PARALYZED THE WHOLE CITY, LEX.
HOW COME SUPERMAN SHOWS UP EVERY TIME A CAT GETS STUCK IN A TREE, BUT HE'S NOWHERE TO BE SEEN WHEN METROPOLIS REALLY NEEDS HIM?
IT'S THE MONSTERS WHICH CONCERN ME MOST, MERCY. THE DEFORMED FREAKS THE ALIEN HAS BROUGHT HERE SINCE HE ARRIVED. THE CREATURES IN THE SUPER-PRISONS...
"...OUR TECHNOLOGY WAS ALL WE HAD TO SUBDUE THEM."
LIVEWIRE? LEMME SEE...
106
LIVEWIRE
WAS SHE THE ONE WHO COULD GOOF AROUND WITH ELECTRICITY AND COMPUTERS AND STUFF, OR AM I THINKING OF SOMEONE ELSE?
YOU GOT IT IN ONE, BOYS.
I'M FLATTERED.

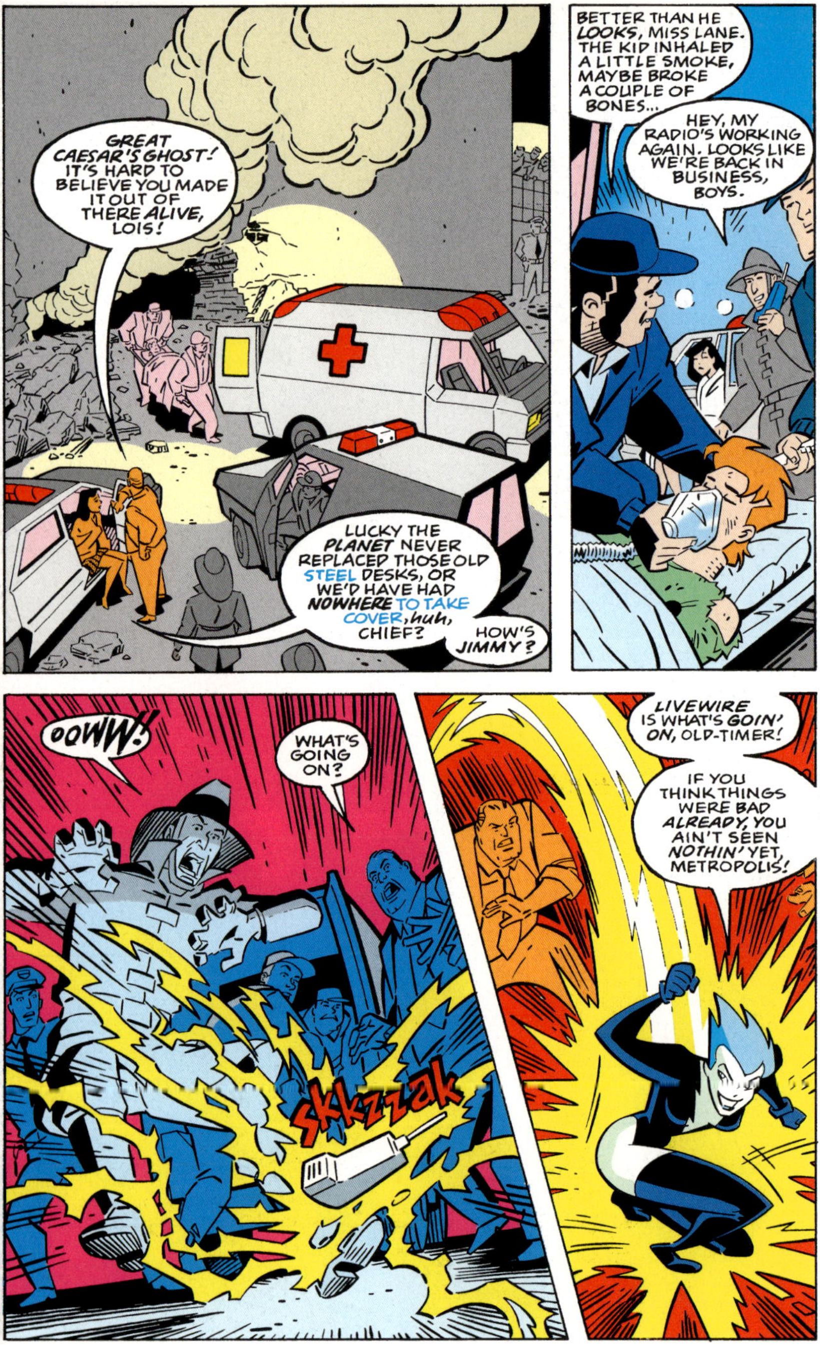
GREAT CAESAR'S GHOST! IT'S HARD TO BELIEVE YOU MADE IT OUT OF THERE ALIVE, LOIS!
LUCKY THE PLANET NEVER REPLACED THOSE OLD STEEL DESKS, OR WE'D HAVE HAD NOWHERE TO TAKE COVER, huh, CHIEF?
HOW'S JIMMY?
BETTER THAN HE LOOKS, MISS LANE. THE KID INHALED A LITTLE SMOKE, MAYBE BROKE A COUPLE OF BONES...
HEY, MY RADIO'S WORKING AGAIN. LOOKS LIKE WE'RE BACK IN BUSINESS, BOYS.
OOWW!
WHAT'S GOING ON?
SKKZZZAK
LIVEWIRE IS WHAT'S GOIN' ON, OLD-TIMER!
IF YOU THINK THINGS WERE BAD ALREADY, YOU AIN'T SEEN NOTHIN' YET, METROPOLIS!

FRANKLY, THAT'S THE KIND OF GARBAGE I'D EXPECT FROM A MALE SUPER-VILLAIN.
OH, PLEASE. SPARE ME THE FEMINIST CRITIQUE FROM THE STEPFORD REPORTER. WRITTEN ANY GOOD PROFILES ABOUT SUPERMAN LATELY, LANE?
WILL YOU GROW UP?
MY FRIEND AND I WERE ALMOST KILLED, SUPERMAN'S GONE MISSING AND BRAINIAC HAS SEIZED CONTROL OF THE WORLD'S NUCLEAR ARSENAL!
DO YOU REALLY THINK THESE PEOPLE CARE WHAT A HIGH-VOLTAGE FORMER SHOCK-JOCK HAS TO SAY?
UH... THIS IS KINDA EMBARRASSING, Y'KNOW?
FOR THE FIRST TIME IN MY LIFE, I'M NOT SURE I CAN THINK OF ANYTHING CLEVER TO SAY...
THEN JUST SAY YOU'LL HELP US.

NINETEEN MINUTES UNTIL THE END OF THE WORLD, PROFESSOR.
YOU ARE MORE RESOURCEFUL THAN YOUR EXTERIOR SUGGESTS, BUT MY EYES AND EARS ARE EVERYWHERE.
YOU WILL BE DEALT WITH SHORTLY.
PLEASE, SUPERMAN, PLEASE FIND A WAY TO HELP ME...
Ah, THERE YOU ARE.
CHOOM!

I BELIEVE KAL-EL USED THIS CHAMBER TO STORE THE WEAPONS HE RETRIEVED FROM HIS CONFLICTS WITH THE WORST EARTH HAD TO OFFER.
IRONIC THAT EVENTS SHOULD END HERE.
DON'T TOUCH THE ORB, BRAINIAC!
THE WEAPON YOU ARE HOLDING IS AN INTERGANG BLASTER, TWO YEARS OLD AND CAPABLE OF ATOMIZING A TANK AT THIS RANGE.
IT WILL NOT EVEN DENT MY CASING, PROFESSOR.
WHOOMP!
WHO SAID I'M AIMING AT YOU?
NO!
SHZZAKK!

YOU...
YOU HAVE NOT STOPPED ME. SEVENTEEN MINUTES UNTIL THE END OF THE WORLD.
SIX MINUTES TO PILOT MY SHIP SAFELY OUT OF RANGE, TWO MINUTES TO BOARD, LEAVING NINE MINUTES ALONE WITH PROFESSOR HAMILTON...
...THIS IS GOING TO BE AN EDUCATION IN ITSELF.
SLAM!
HRRK!
GAARRGH!
KZZZRRK
GET OUT! GET OUT OF MY HEAD!
S-SUPERMAN...?

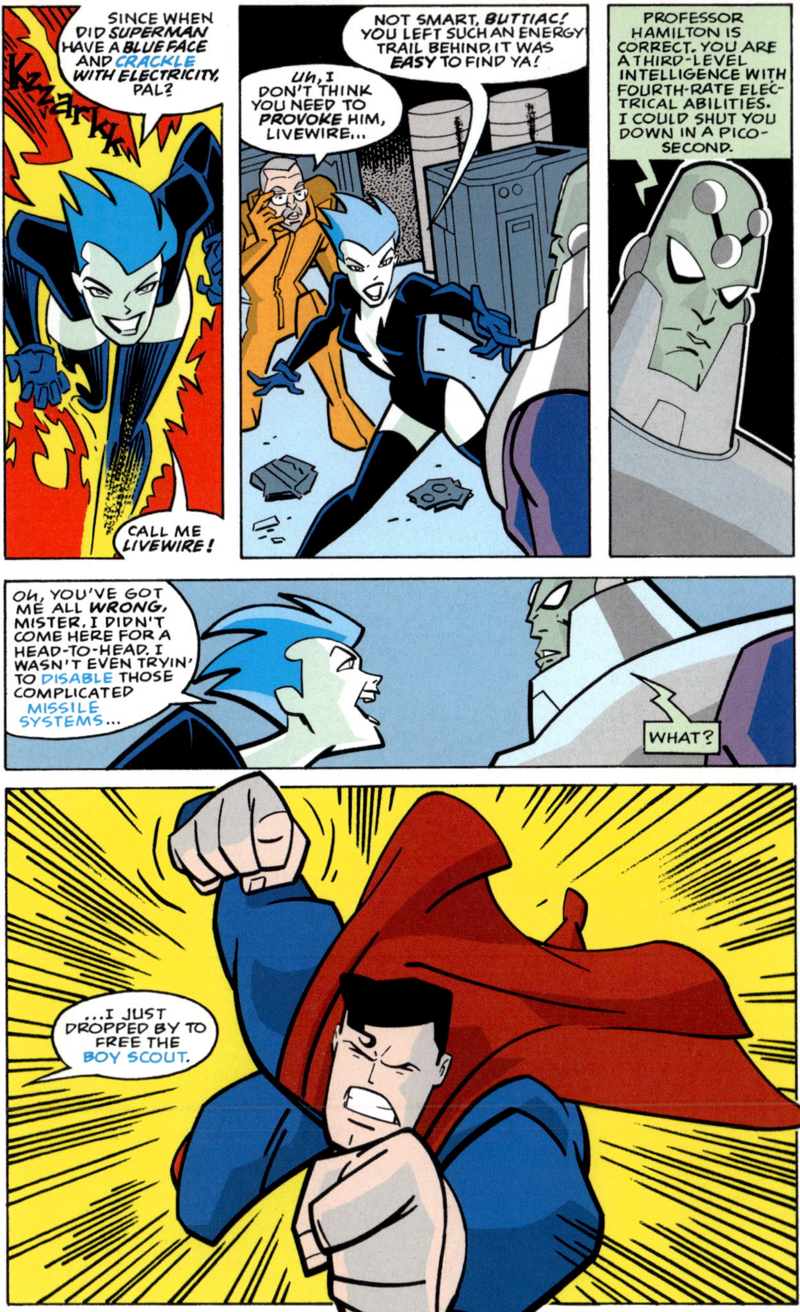
SINCE WHEN DID SUPERMAN HAVE A BLUE FACE AND CRACKLE WITH ELECTRICITY, PAL?
KZZARKK
CALL ME LIVEWIRE!
NOT SMART, BUTTIAC! YOU LEFT SUCH AN ENERGY TRAIL BEHIND, IT WAS EASY TO FIND YA!
UH, I DON'T THINK YOU NEED TO PROVOKE HIM, LIVEWIRE...
PROFESSOR HAMILTON IS CORRECT. YOU ARE A THIRD-LEVEL INTELLIGENCE WITH FOURTH-RATE ELECTRICAL ABILITIES. I COULD SHUT YOU DOWN IN A PICO-SECOND.
OH, YOU'VE GOT ME ALL WRONG, MISTER. I DIDN'T COME HERE FOR A HEAD-TO-HEAD. I WASN'T EVEN TRYIN' TO DISABLE THOSE COMPLICATED MISSILE SYSTEMS...
WHAT?
...I JUST DROPPED BY TO FREE THE BOY SCOUT.

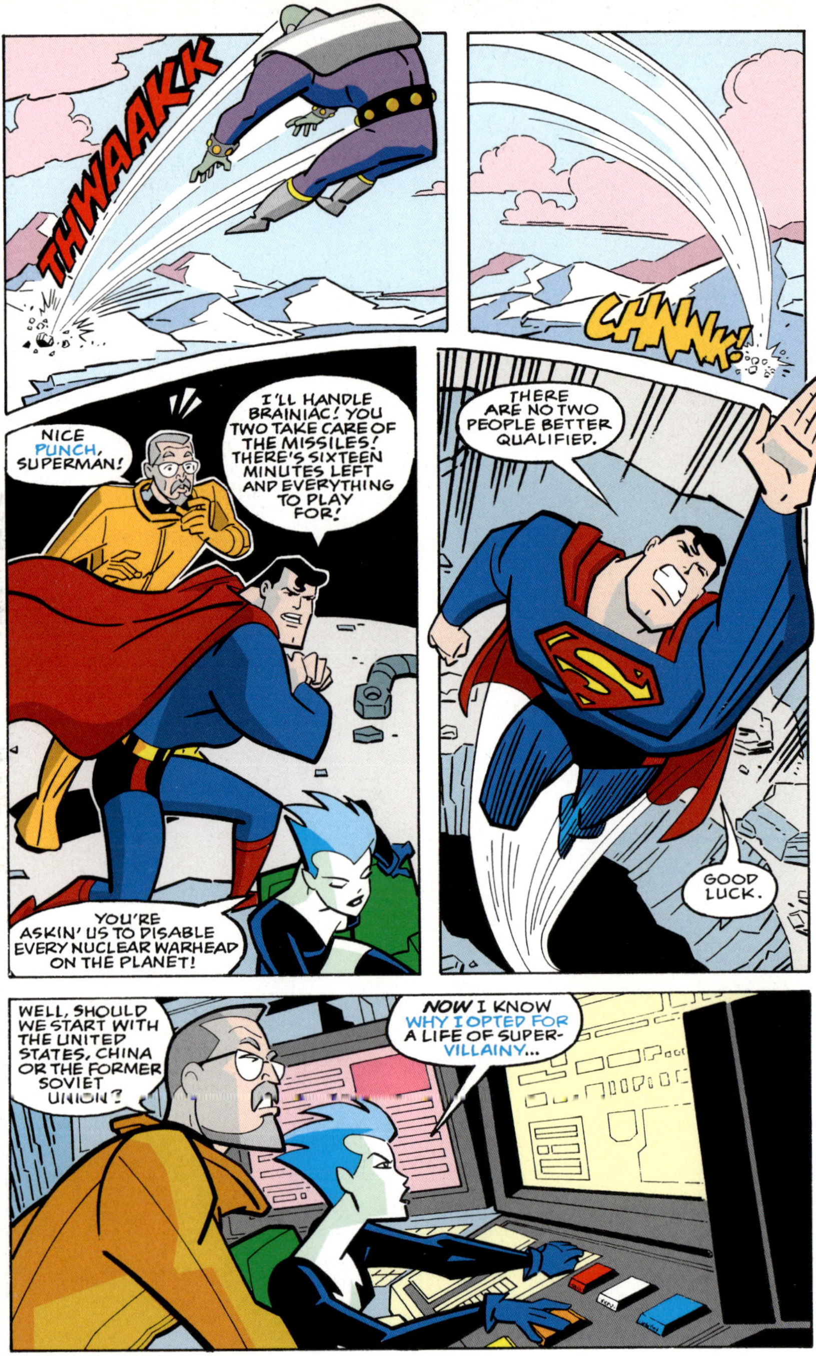
THWAAKK
CHNNK!
NICE PUNCH, SUPERMAN!
I'LL HANDLE BRAINIAC! YOU TWO TAKE CARE OF THE MISSILES! THERE'S SIXTEEN MINUTES LEFT AND EVERYTHING TO PLAY FOR!
YOU'RE ASKIN' US TO DISABLE EVERY NUCLEAR WARHEAD ON THE PLANET!
THERE ARE NO TWO PEOPLE BETTER QUALIFIED.
GOOD LUCK.
WELL, SHOULD WE START WITH THE UNITED STATES, CHINA OR THE FORMER SOVIET UNION?
NOW I KNOW WHY I OPTED FOR A LIFE OF SUPER-VILLAINY...

YOU ALREADY TOOK KRYPTON FROM ME, BRAINIAC! I WON'T LET YOU DO THE SAME TO EARTH!
KRUNNK!
Thwakk
HOW DARE YOU THREATEN MY WORLD LIKE THIS?
HOW
DARE
YOU?
KPOWW!

WE STILL HAVE THIRTEEN MINUTES LEFT TO STOP THOSE MISSILES AND SAVE THE LIVES OF FIVE BILLION PEOPLE.
YOU CAN EITHER DO THE DECENT THING, OR DIE WITH THE REST OF US, BECAUSE YOU'RE NOT LEAVING EARTH.
ON THE CONTRARY, KAL-EL...
I AM DESERTING THIS BACTERIAL ROCK IN A MATTER OF MINUTES FOR MORE CIVIL-IZED CULTURES I MIGHT RECORD AND EXTERMINATE.
BEFORE I GO, THERE ARE ONE OR TWO DETAILS I MUST ATTEND TO...
GREAT SCOTT...!
...THE FIRST OF WHICH IS DELETING YOU.

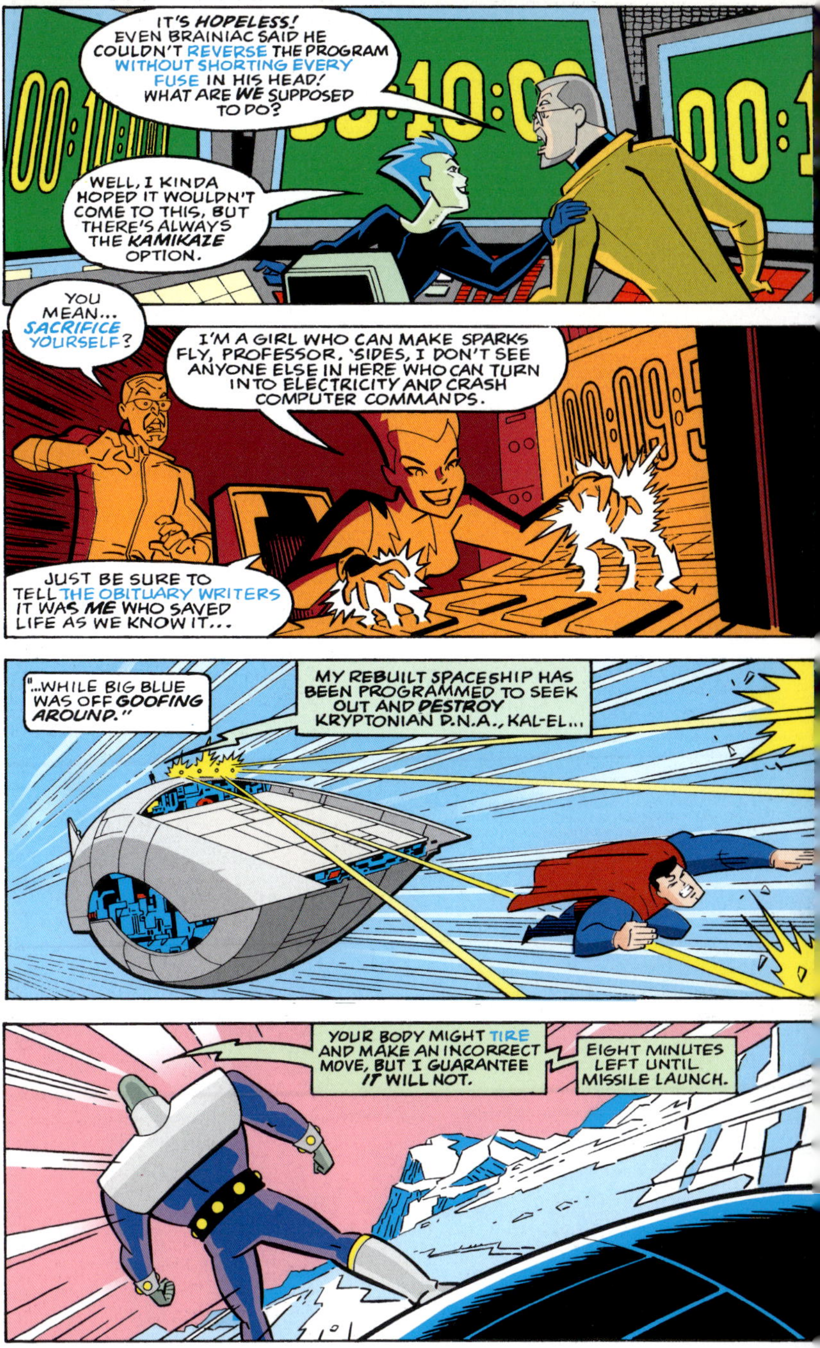

IT'S HOPELESS! EVEN BRAINIAC SAID HE COULDN'T REVERSE THE PROGRAM WITHOUT SHORTING EVERY FUSE IN HIS HEAD! WHAT ARE WE SUPPOSED TO DO?
WELL, I KINDA HOPED IT WOULDN'T COME TO THIS, BUT THERE'S ALWAYS THE KAMIKAZE OPTION.
YOU MEAN... SACRIFICE YOURSELF?
I'M A GIRL WHO CAN MAKE SPARKS FLY, PROFESSOR. 'SIDES, I DON'T SEE ANYONE ELSE IN HERE WHO CAN TURN INTO ELECTRICITY AND CRASH COMPUTER COMMANDS.
JUST BE SURE TO TELL THE OBITUARY WRITERS IT WAS ME WHO SAVED LIFE AS WE KNOW IT...
"...WHILE BIG BLUE WAS OFF GOOFING AROUND."
MY REBUILT SPACESHIP HAS BEEN PROGRAMMED TO SEEK OUT AND DESTROY KRYPTONIAN D.N.A., KAL-EL...
YOUR BODY MIGHT TIRE AND MAKE AN INCORRECT MOVE, BUT I GUARANTEE IT WILL NOT.
EIGHT MINUTES LEFT UNTIL MISSILE LAUNCH.

MORE THAN ENOUGH TIME TO RETRIEVE THE KRYPTONIAN ORB AND DELETE THE TWO REMAINING LIFE-FORMS.
ALTHOUGH WHY LIVEWIRE, FILED UNDER META-CRIMINALS, CHOSE TO RESCUE KAL-EL FROM THE PHANTOM ZONE IS A STEP IN LOGIC I AM UNABLE TO COMPUTE.
BECAUSE SHE'S HUMAN, BRAINIAC! SOMETHING ALL THE DATA IN THE UNIVERSE COULDN'T MAKE YOU UNDERSTAND!
BY THE WAY, SETTING YOUR SHIP TO TRACK MY D.N.A....
...WAS A STUPID MISTAKE FOR A TWELFTH-LEVEL INTELLIGENCE!
BA-BOOM!
KZZAKK!
DEAR GOD!
AAAUUUGGH!

"YOU DID IT! YOU ACTUALLY DID IT!
SPORT WEAR
SALES
"THE POWER'S COMING BACK STATE BY STATE!
"I'M GETTING READINGS FROM ALL ACROSS THE COUNTRY! THE MISSILES ARE STAYING WHERE THEY ARE!
"YOU'VE SAVED THE WORLD, LIVEWIRE!"
YOU'VE...
LIVEWIRE?
IT'S OVER, BRAINIAC. MY SUPER-HEARING TELLS ME THAT LIVEWIRE STOPPED THE MISSILES.
ALL THAT'S LEFT TO DO NOW IS BURY YOUR CENTRAL PROCESSOR AT THE BOTTOM OF THE MARIANAS TRENCH.
SHE NEUTRALIZED EVERY MISSILE EXCEPT ONE, KAL-EL.
WHAT...?
AN INTERCONTINENTAL BALLISTIC MISSILE, HEADING STRAIGHT FOR THE HEART OF METROPOLIS

"...MY ESCAPE PLAN."
OF COURSE, WE COULD RESUME COMBAT, BUT VICTORY IS NO GUARANTEE, AND IT'S KNOWN THROUGHOUT THE WORLD YOU REGARD THAT CITY WITH SOME AFFECTION.
YOUR CHOICE--
--SEEMS CLEAR.
BLAST IT!
AS CALCULATED.
I WILL RETURN SHORTLY, LAST SON OF KRYPTON, WITH AN UPGRADE. I SUGGEST YOU BEGIN PREPARATIONS.

THE COUNTRY'S BACK ON FULL POWER, MISTER PRESIDENT, BUT THIS ISN'T OVER BY A LONG SHOT.
GENERAL HARDCASTLE'S ON THE LINE...
OUR BIRDS ARE PERCHED IN THEIR SILOS, SIR, BUT A SOVIET I.C.B.M. HAS FLOWN THE COOP. IT LOOKS LIKE IT'S HEADING IN OUR DIRECTION!
METROPOLIS...
...WHY IS IT ALWAYS METROPOLIS?
"DEAR LORD, IF WE EVER NEEDED A MIRACLE...
"...NOW'S THE TIME."

LOOK, BOSS! IT'S SUPERMAN!
HNN!
AT LEAST TRY TO PRETEND YOU AREN'T PLEASED TO SEE HIM, MERCY. FOR MY SAKE.
EVERYBODY DOWN!
THIS...
WOW!
...IS GONNA... BE CLOSE...
HEY, WHERE'S HE TAKING IT?
WHERE DO YOU THINK...?

"...UP, UP AND AWAY."
COMPUTER, SET A COURSE FOR ALPHA CENTAURI.
THERE IS A STERILE WORLD IN THAT SYSTEM WE CAN ASSIMILATE WHILE WE UPGRADE AND DEVISE A STRATEGY FOR OUR VICTORIOUS RETURN TO EARTH.
BRAINIAC, INTERFACE WITH THE RADAR SCREENS...
THERE IS SOMETHING DIFFICULT TO IDENTIFY HEADING IN OUR DIRECTION.
NO.
GOTCHA.

Vokabelerklärungen (S. 92–101)

S. 92/93
debris [dəˈbrih] Schutt
you endangered … [ju inˈdäindschərd] du hast … in Gefahr gebracht
laughing stock [ˈlähfing stahk] Witzfigur
sentient [ˈßenschənt] empfindungsfähig
mischief [ˈmißtschəf] Unfug

S. 94/95
parachute [ˈpärəschuht] Fallschirm
by honking a horn [bai ˈhahnking ə hohrn] indem ich hupe
remedied [ˈremədihd] behoben
Guilty as charged! [ˈgilti äs tschahrdschd] Schuldig in allen Punkten der Anklage!
deserves to lose 'em (= them) [diˈsöhrvs tə luhs əm] verdient, sie zu verlieren
trust [traßt] vertrauen

S. 96/97
ergs [örgs] Einheiten
humiliating you [hjuhˈmiljäiting ju] dich zu demütigen
spit-curl [ˈßbitköhrl] Schmalzlocke
butt [bat] Hintern
antagonize [änˈtägənais] reizen
Darn straight! [darn ßträit] Verdammt richtig!
one thing I can't stand [wan θing ai kahnt ßtänd] eine Sache, die ich nicht ausstehen kann
morons yelling at me [ˈmorəns ˈjeling ət mih] Schwachköpfe, die mich anschreien

S. 98/99
on my whim [ahn mai wim] nach meiner Laune
dump [damp] Drecknest
leap [lihp] überspringen
bound [baund] Sprung/Satz

S. 100/101
dubbed [dabd] taufte
reign [räin] Herrschaft
under siege [ˈandər ßihdsch] im Belagerungszustand
drain [dräin] entziehen
disappear [dißəˈpihr] verschwinden
resigning issue [riˈsaining ˈischuh] ein Zeichen dafür, dass er aufgibt
jailbreak [ˈdschäilbräik] Gefängnisausbruch
theft [θeft] Diebstahl
flu bug [fluh bag] Grippebazillus
leads [lihds] Anhaltspunkte
every time he busts out of prison [ˈevri taim hi baßtß aut əv ˈprisən] jedes Mal, wenn er aus dem Gefängnis ausbricht

► *Nächste Ausklappseite: S. 111*

Vokabelerklärungen (S. 82–91)

S. 82/83
how dare you threaten my world [hau der ju θretn mai wöhrld] wie kannst du es wagen, meine Welt zu bedrohen
decent [dihßnt] anständig/ehrbar
I am deserting [ai əm diˈsöhrting] ich verlasse
exterminate [ixˈtöhrminäit] ausrotten
I must attend to [ai maßt əˈtend tə] um die ich mich kümmern muss

S. 84/85
reverse [riˈvöhrß] rückgängig machen
without shorting every fuse [wiðˈaut ˈschohrting ˈevri fjuhs] ohne sämtliche Sicherungen durchbrennen zu lassen
sacrifice yourself [ˈßäkrifaiß jurˈßelf] dich opfern
the obituary writers [ði əˈbitschuəri ˈraitərs] den Verfassern des Nachrufs
tire [ˈtaiər] ermüden
filed under [faild ˈandər] die einzuordnen ist als
compute [kamˈpjuht] errechnen
human [ˈhjuhmən] ein menschliches Wesen
to track [tə träk] um aufzuspüren/zu verfolgen

S. 86/87
bury [ˈberi] begraben
at the bottom [ät ðə ˈbahtəm] auf dem Grund
Marianas Trench [märiˈjähnəs trentsch] Mariannengraben
except [iˈxept] außer
escape plan [ißˈkäip plän] Fluchtplan
resume combat [riˈßjuhm ˈkahmbät] den Kampf wieder aufnehmen
affection [əˈfekschn] Zuneigung
Your choice. [jur tschoiß] Du hast die Wahl.
Blast it! [bläßt it] Verdammt!

S. 88/89
are perched [ahr pöhrtscht] sitzen
it's heading in our direction [itß ˈheding in auər diˈrekschən] sie steuert auf uns zu
to pretend [tə priˈtend] so zu tun als ob
for my sake [fohr mai ßäik] mir zuliebe
close [klouß] knapp

S. 90/91
devise a strategy [diˈvais ə ˈßträtədschi] eine Strategie entwickeln
victorious [vikˈtohriəß] siegreich
Gotcha! (= Got you!) [ˈgahtschə] Hab dich!
perkier [ˈpöhrkiər] munterer
if she recovers [if schi riˈkavərs] wenn sie sich wieder erholt

▶ *Nächste Ausklappseite: S. 92*

POWER CORRUPTS, SUPER POWER CORRUPTS ABSOLUTELY!
MARK MILLAR - WRITER
ALUIR AMANCIO - PENCILLER
TERRY AUSTIN - INKER
MARIE SEVERIN - COLORIST
LOIS BUHALIS - LETTERER
FRANK BERRIOS - ASSISTANT
MIKE MCAVENNIE - EDITOR
SUPERMAN CREATED BY Jerry Siegel & Joe Shuster
HELP ME!

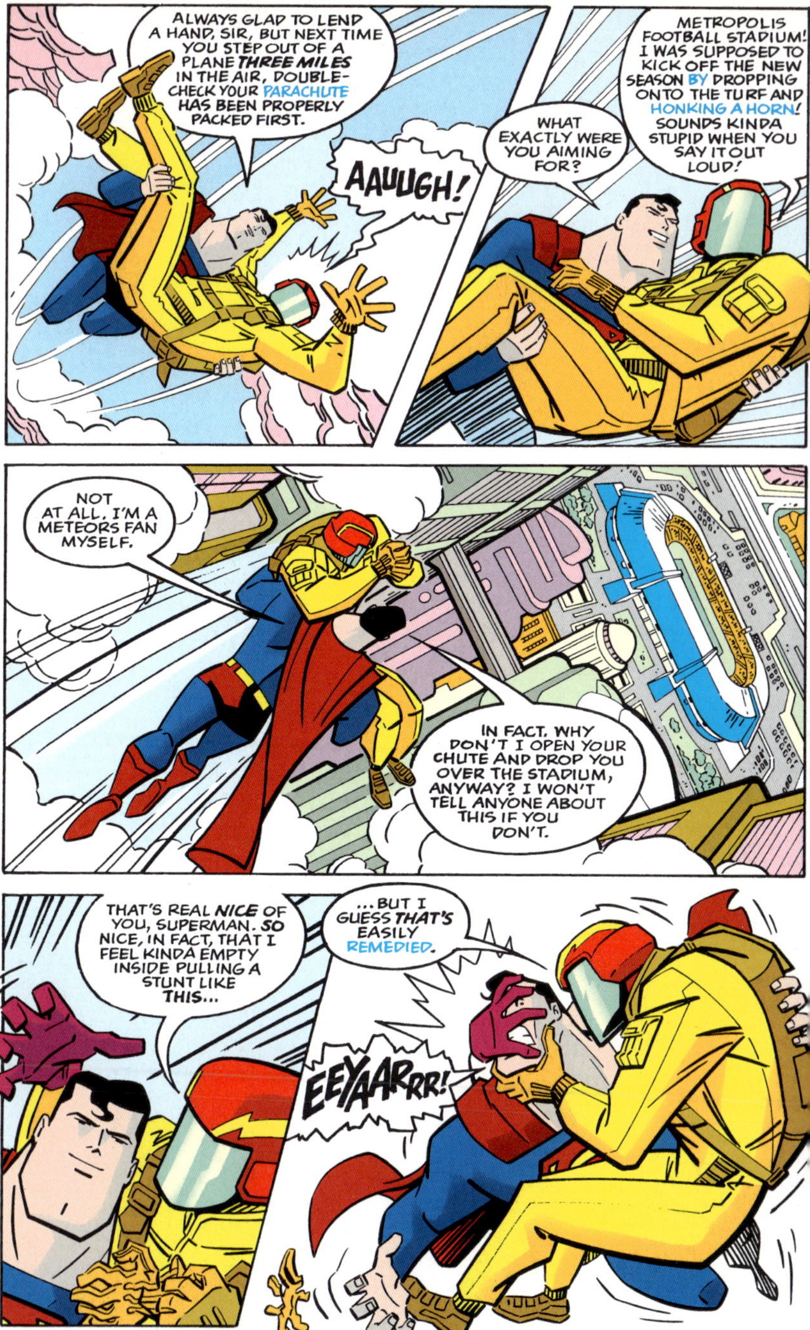
ALWAYS GLAD TO LEND A HAND, SIR, BUT NEXT TIME YOU STEP OUT OF A PLANE **THREE MILES** IN THE AIR, DOUBLE-CHECK YOUR PARACHUTE HAS BEEN PROPERLY PACKED FIRST.
AAUUGH!
METROPOLIS FOOTBALL STADIUM! I WAS SUPPOSED TO KICK OFF THE NEW SEASON BY DROPPING ONTO THE TURF AND HONKING A HORN! SOUNDS KINDA STUPID WHEN YOU SAY IT OUT LOUD!
WHAT EXACTLY WERE YOU AIMING FOR?
NOT AT ALL, I'M A METEORS FAN MYSELF.
IN FACT, WHY DON'T I OPEN YOUR CHUTE AND DROP YOU OVER THE STADIUM, ANYWAY? I WON'T TELL ANYONE ABOUT THIS IF YOU DON'T.
THAT'S REAL **NICE** OF YOU, SUPERMAN. **SO** NICE, IN FACT, THAT I FEEL KINDA EMPTY INSIDE PULLING A STUNT LIKE **THIS...**
...BUT I GUESS **THAT'S** EASILY REMEDIED.
EEYAARRR!

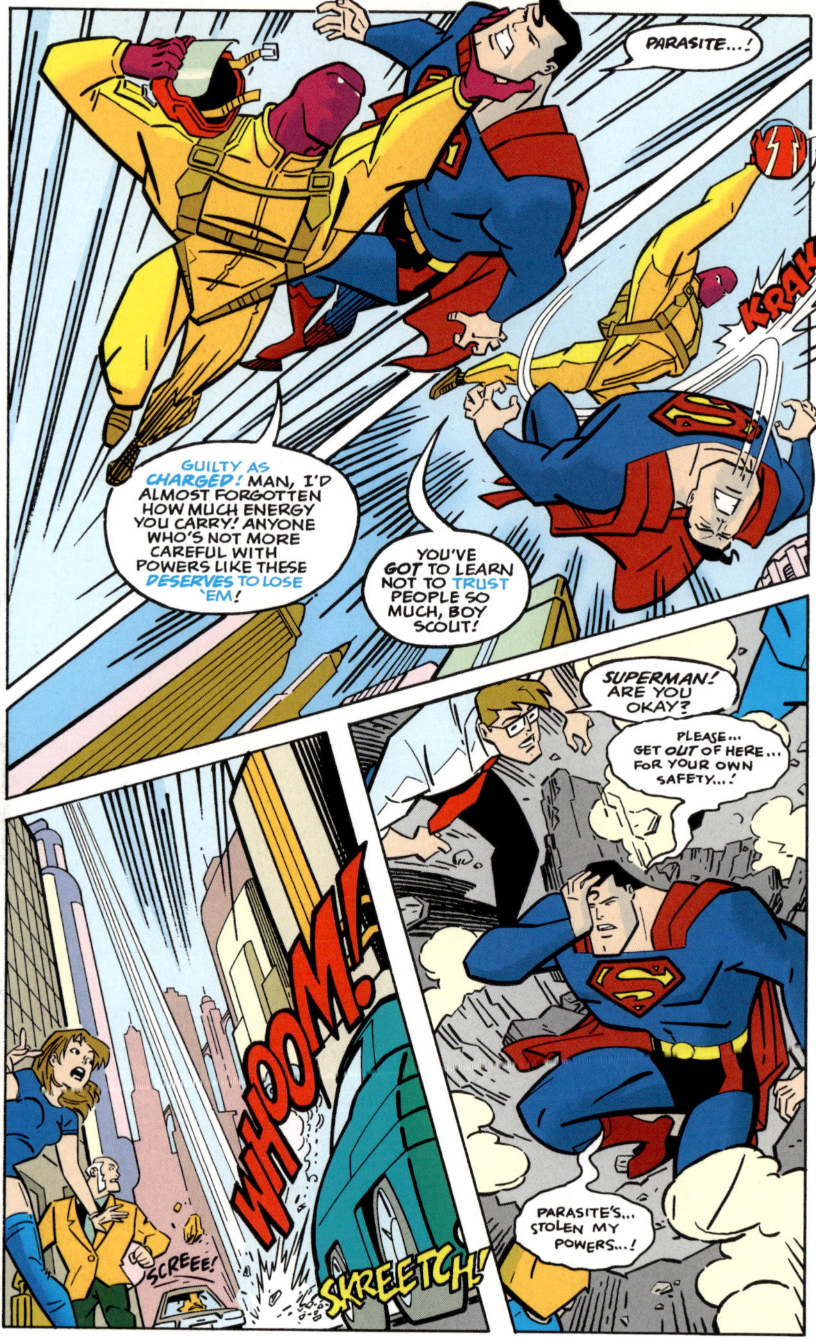

PARASITE...!
KRAK
GUILTY AS CHARGED! MAN, I'D ALMOST FORGOTTEN HOW MUCH ENERGY YOU CARRY! ANYONE WHO'S NOT MORE CAREFUL WITH POWERS LIKE THESE DESERVES TO LOSE 'EM!
YOU'VE GOT TO LEARN NOT TO TRUST PEOPLE SO MUCH, BOY SCOUT!
SUPERMAN! ARE YOU OKAY?
PLEASE... GET OUT OF HERE... FOR YOUR OWN SAFETY...!
PARASITE'S... STOLEN MY POWERS...!
WHOOM!
SCREEE!
SKREETCH!

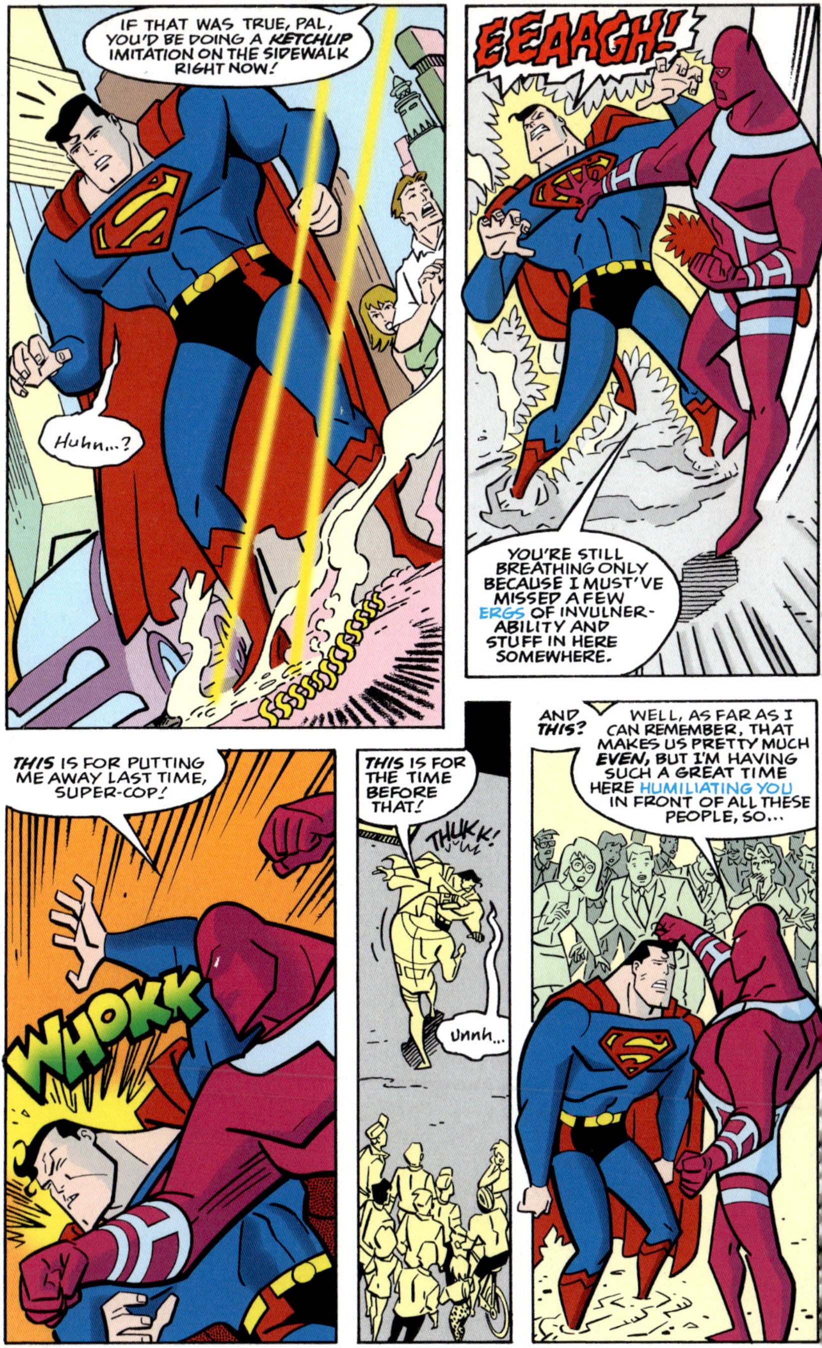
IF THAT WAS TRUE, PAL, YOU'D BE DOING A KETCHUP IMITATION ON THE SIDEWALK RIGHT NOW!
Huhn...?
EEAAGH!
YOU'RE STILL BREATHING ONLY BECAUSE I MUST'VE MISSED A FEW ERGS OF INVULNER-ABILITY AND STUFF IN HERE SOMEWHERE.
THIS IS FOR PUTTING ME AWAY LAST TIME, SUPER-COP!
WHOKK
THIS IS FOR THE TIME BEFORE THAT!
THUKK!
Unnh...
AND THIS?
WELL, AS FAR AS I CAN REMEMBER, THAT MAKES US PRETTY MUCH EVEN, BUT I'M HAVING SUCH A GREAT TIME HERE HUMILIATING YOU IN FRONT OF ALL THESE PEOPLE, SO...

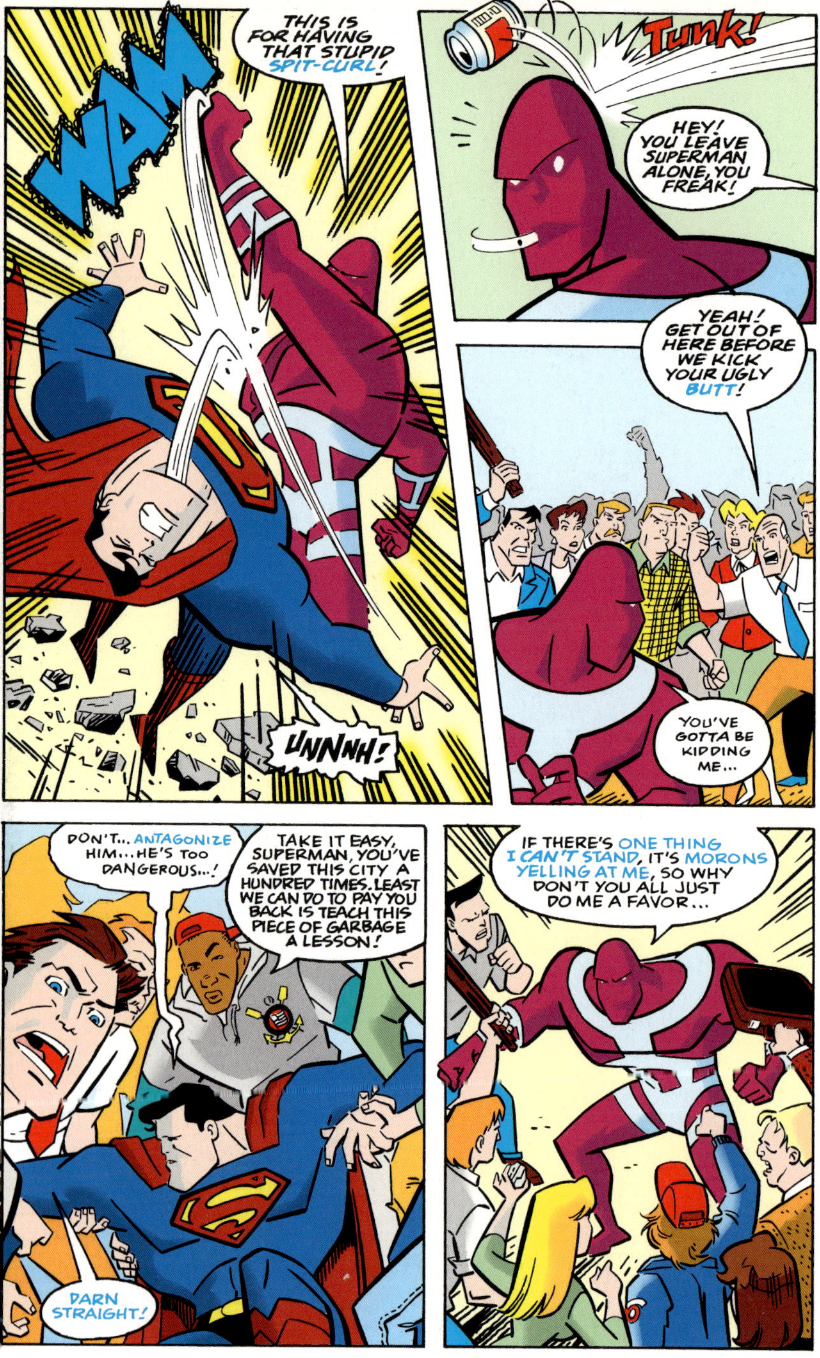
THIS IS FOR HAVING THAT STUPID SPIT-CURL!
WAM
UNNNH!
Tunk!
HEY! YOU LEAVE SUPERMAN ALONE, YOU FREAK!
YEAH! GET OUT OF HERE BEFORE WE KICK YOUR UGLY BUTT!
YOU'VE GOTTA BE KIDDING ME...
DON'T... ANTAGONIZE HIM... HE'S TOO DANGEROUS...!
TAKE IT EASY, SUPERMAN, YOU'VE SAVED THIS CITY A HUNDRED TIMES. LEAST WE CAN DO TO PAY YOU BACK IS TEACH THIS PIECE OF GARBAGE A LESSON!
DARN STRAIGHT!
IF THERE'S ONE THING I CAN'T STAND, IT'S MORONS YELLING AT ME, SO WHY DON'T YOU ALL JUST DO ME A FAVOR...

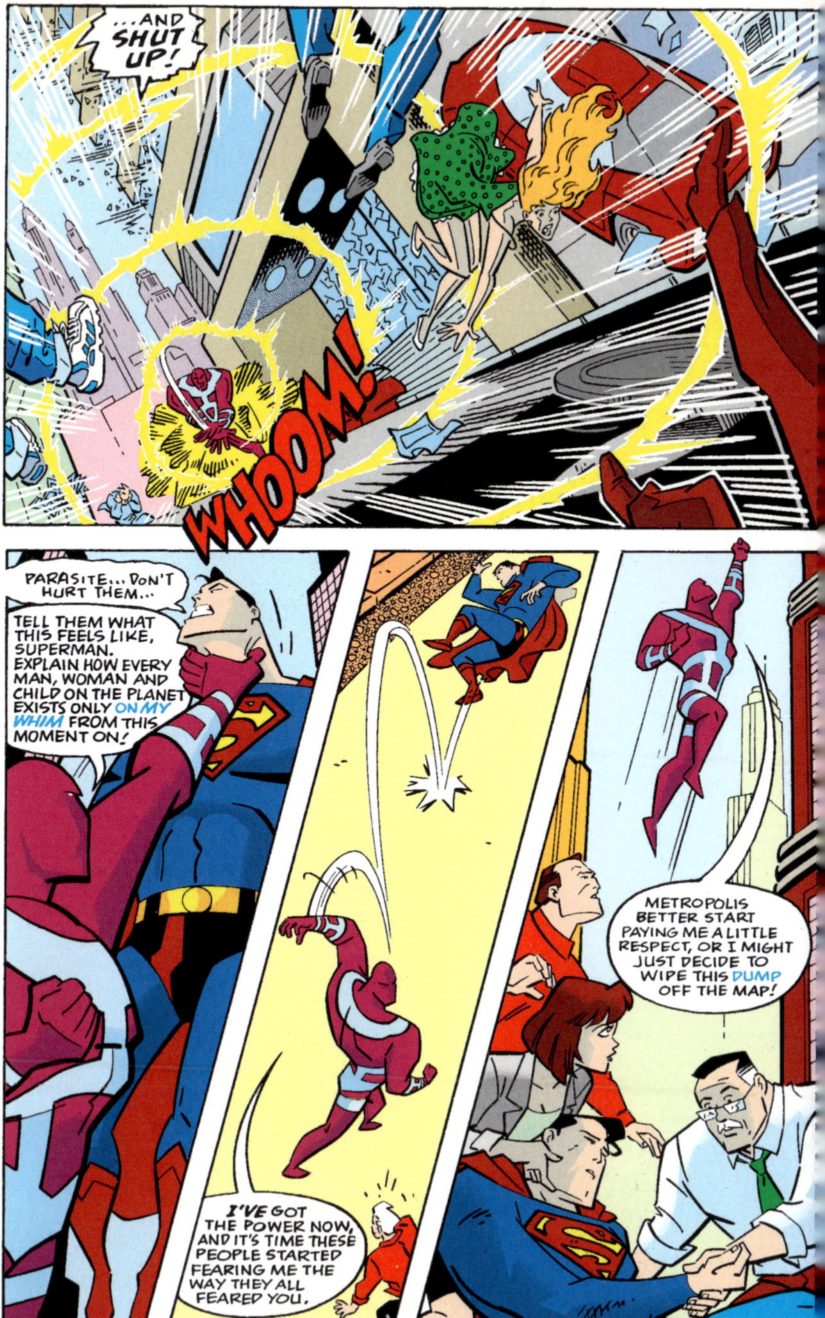
...AND SHUT UP!
WHOOM!
PARASITE... DON'T HURT THEM...
TELL THEM WHAT THIS FEELS LIKE, SUPERMAN. EXPLAIN HOW EVERY MAN, WOMAN AND CHILD ON THE PLANET EXISTS ONLY ON MY WHIM FROM THIS MOMENT ON!
I'VE GOT THE POWER NOW, AND IT'S TIME THESE PEOPLE STARTED FEARING ME THE WAY THEY ALL FEARED YOU.
METROPOLIS BETTER START PAYING ME A LITTLE RESPECT, OR I MIGHT JUST DECIDE TO WIPE THIS DUMP OFF THE MAP!

FASTER THAN A SPEEDING BULLET!
MORE POWERFUL THAN A LOCOMOTIVE!
ABLE TO LEAP TALL BUILDINGS IN A SINGLE BOUND!
NOT A BIRD, NOT A PLANE, AND DEFINITELY NOT SUPERMAN!

RUDY JONES, THE MAN THE MEDIA DUBBED THE PARASITE AFTER A HORRIFIC INDUS-TRIAL ACCIDENT, HAS BROUGHT METROPOLIS TO ITS KNEES IN A REIGN OF TERROR, SO FAR LASTING TWENTY-FOUR HOURS.
HOW MUCH LONGER WILL THE CITY REMAIN UNDER SIEGE? THE WARDEN AT STRYKER'S ISLAND HAD THIS ANSWER:
Angela Ch
LT938
89
THE PARASITE IS AN ENERGY VAMPIRE. HE NEEDS TO DRAIN THE LIFE FORCE FROM HIS VICTIMS ON A REGULAR BASIS OR HIS POWERS DISAPPEAR WITHIN TWO TO THREE DAYS.
AS FOR WHETHER HIS ESCAPE IS A RESIGNING ISSUE, I HAVE TO SAY THE ANSWER IS A DEFINITE NO.
INCOMPETENCE OR OTHERWISE, THE PARASITE JAILBREAK AND SUBSEQUENT THEFT OF SUPERMAN'S POWERS MAY PUSH THE CITY'S CRIME RATE TO AN ALL-TIME HIGH.
LEX LUTHOR, CHAIRMAN OF LEXCORP INTERNATIONAL.
SUPERMAN'S CARELESSNESS WITH HIS SPECIAL ABILITIES HAS RESULTED IN THE CLEARANCE OF ALMOST EVERY BANK VAULT IN THE CITY, AND THE HOSPITALIZATION OF HALF THE SPECIAL CRIMES UNIT.

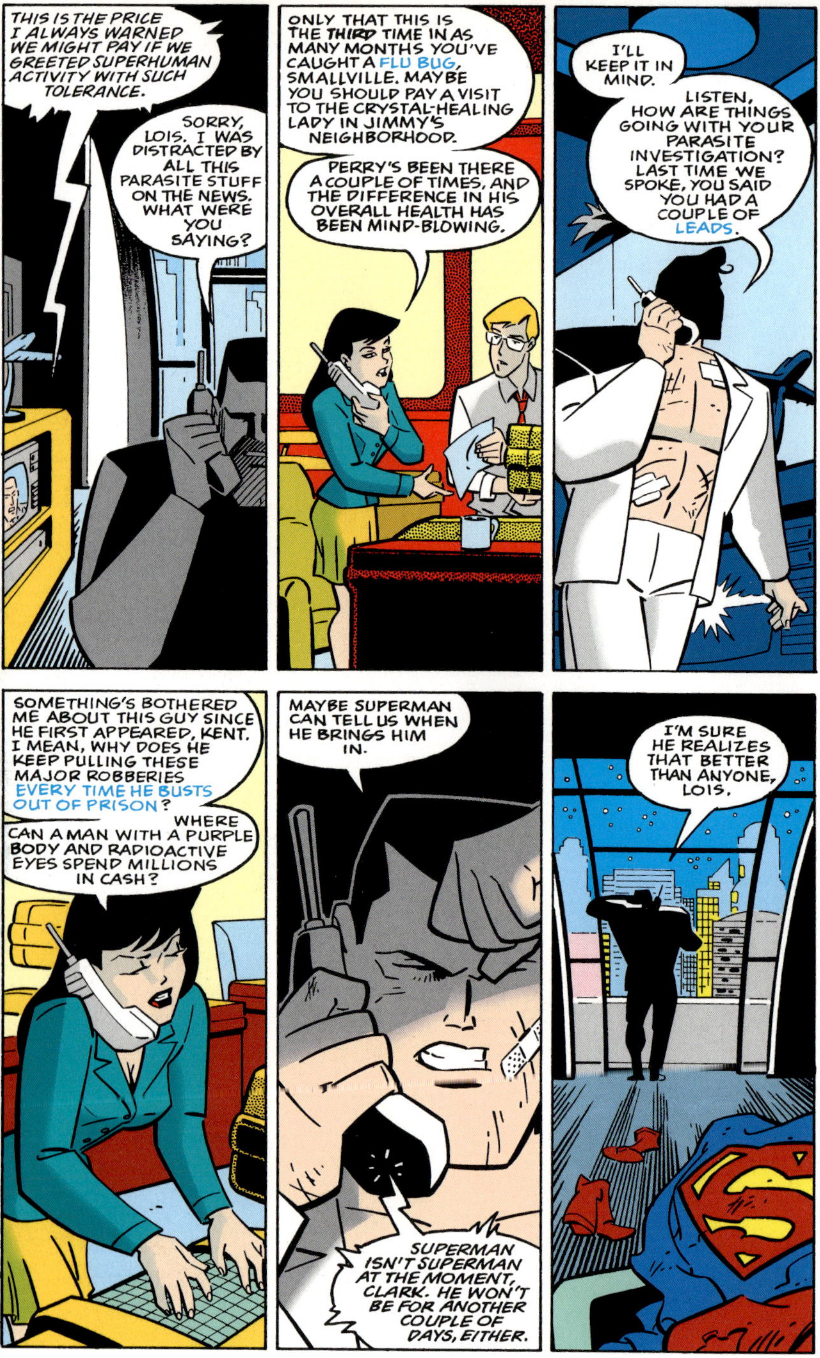
THIS IS THE PRICE I ALWAYS WARNED WE MIGHT PAY IF WE GREETED SUPERHUMAN ACTIVITY WITH SUCH TOLERANCE.
SORRY, LOIS. I WAS DISTRACTED BY ALL THIS PARASITE STUFF ON THE NEWS. WHAT WERE YOU SAYING?
ONLY THAT THIS IS THE THIRD TIME IN AS MANY MONTHS YOU'VE CAUGHT A FLU BUG, SMALLVILLE. MAYBE YOU SHOULD PAY A VISIT TO THE CRYSTAL-HEALING LADY IN JIMMY'S NEIGHBORHOOD.
PERRY'S BEEN THERE A COUPLE OF TIMES, AND THE DIFFERENCE IN HIS OVERALL HEALTH HAS BEEN MIND-BLOWING.
I'LL KEEP IT IN MIND.
LISTEN, HOW ARE THINGS GOING WITH YOUR PARASITE INVESTIGATION? LAST TIME WE SPOKE, YOU SAID YOU HAD A COUPLE OF LEADS.
SOMETHING'S BOTHERED ME ABOUT THIS GUY SINCE HE FIRST APPEARED, KENT. I MEAN, WHY DOES HE KEEP PULLING THESE MAJOR ROBBERIES EVERY TIME HE BUSTS OUT OF PRISON?
WHERE CAN A MAN WITH A PURPLE BODY AND RADIOACTIVE EYES SPEND MILLIONS IN CASH?
MAYBE SUPERMAN CAN TELL US WHEN HE BRINGS HIM IN.
SUPERMAN ISN'T SUPERMAN AT THE MOMENT, CLARK. HE WON'T BE FOR ANOTHER COUPLE OF DAYS, EITHER.
I'M SURE HE REALIZES THAT BETTER THAN ANYONE, LOIS.

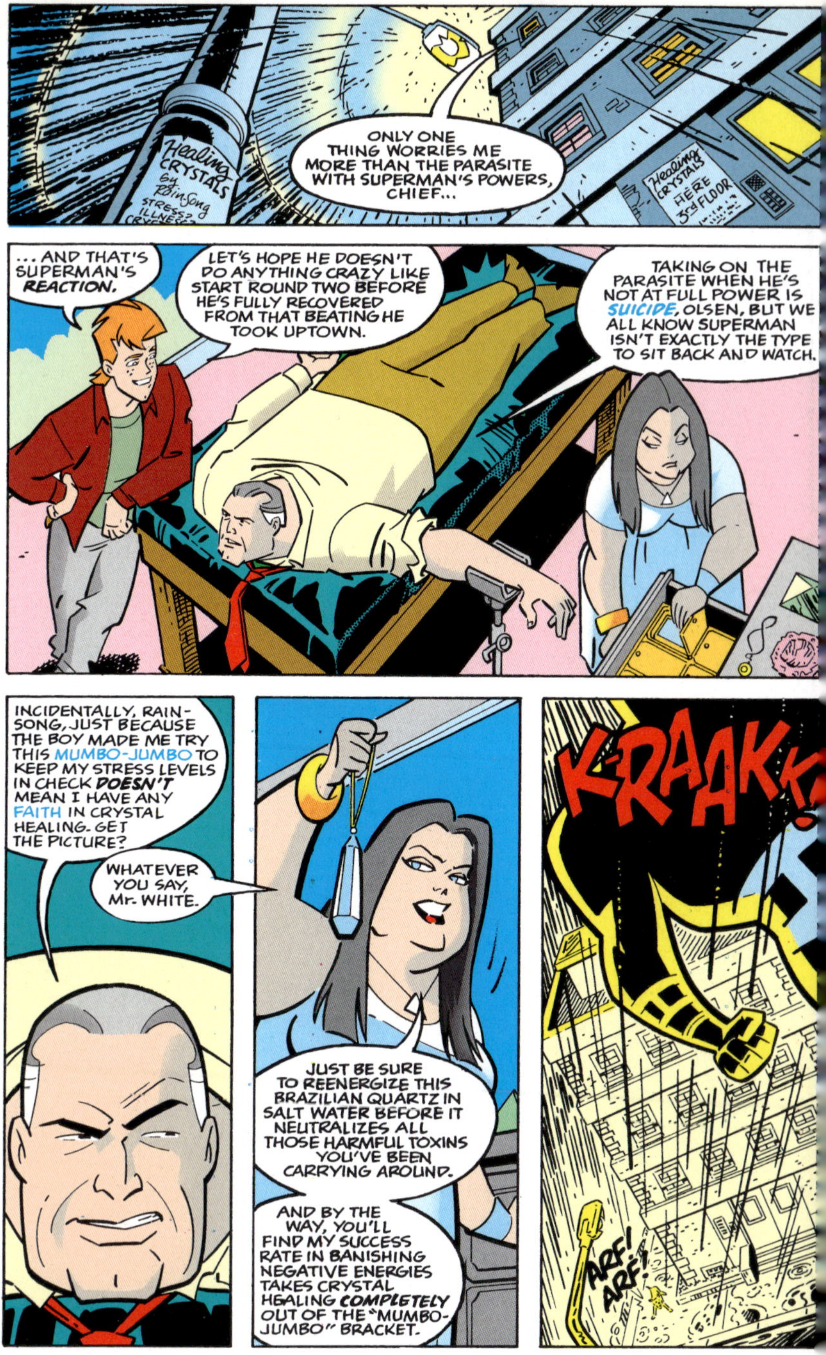
Healing CRYSTALS by RainSong STRESS? ILLNESS?
ONLY ONE THING WORRIES ME MORE THAN THE PARASITE WITH SUPERMAN'S POWERS, CHIEF...
Healing CRYSTALS HERE 3rd FLOOR
... AND THAT'S SUPERMAN'S REACTION.
LET'S HOPE HE DOESN'T DO ANYTHING CRAZY LIKE START ROUND TWO BEFORE HE'S FULLY RECOVERED FROM THAT BEATING HE TOOK UPTOWN.
TAKING ON THE PARASITE WHEN HE'S NOT AT FULL POWER IS SUICIDE, OLSEN, BUT WE ALL KNOW SUPERMAN ISN'T EXACTLY THE TYPE TO SIT BACK AND WATCH.
INCIDENTALLY, RAIN-SONG, JUST BECAUSE THE BOY MADE ME TRY THIS MUMBO-JUMBO TO KEEP MY STRESS LEVELS IN CHECK DOESN'T MEAN I HAVE ANY FAITH IN CRYSTAL HEALING. GET THE PICTURE?
WHATEVER YOU SAY, Mr. WHITE.
JUST BE SURE TO REENERGIZE THIS BRAZILIAN QUARTZ IN SALT WATER BEFORE IT NEUTRALIZES ALL THOSE HARMFUL TOXINS YOU'VE BEEN CARRYING AROUND.
AND BY THE WAY, YOU'LL FIND MY SUCCESS RATE IN BANISHING NEGATIVE ENERGIES TAKES CRYSTAL HEALING COMPLETELY OUT OF THE "MUMBO-JUMBO" BRACKET.
K-RAAKK!
ARF! ARF!

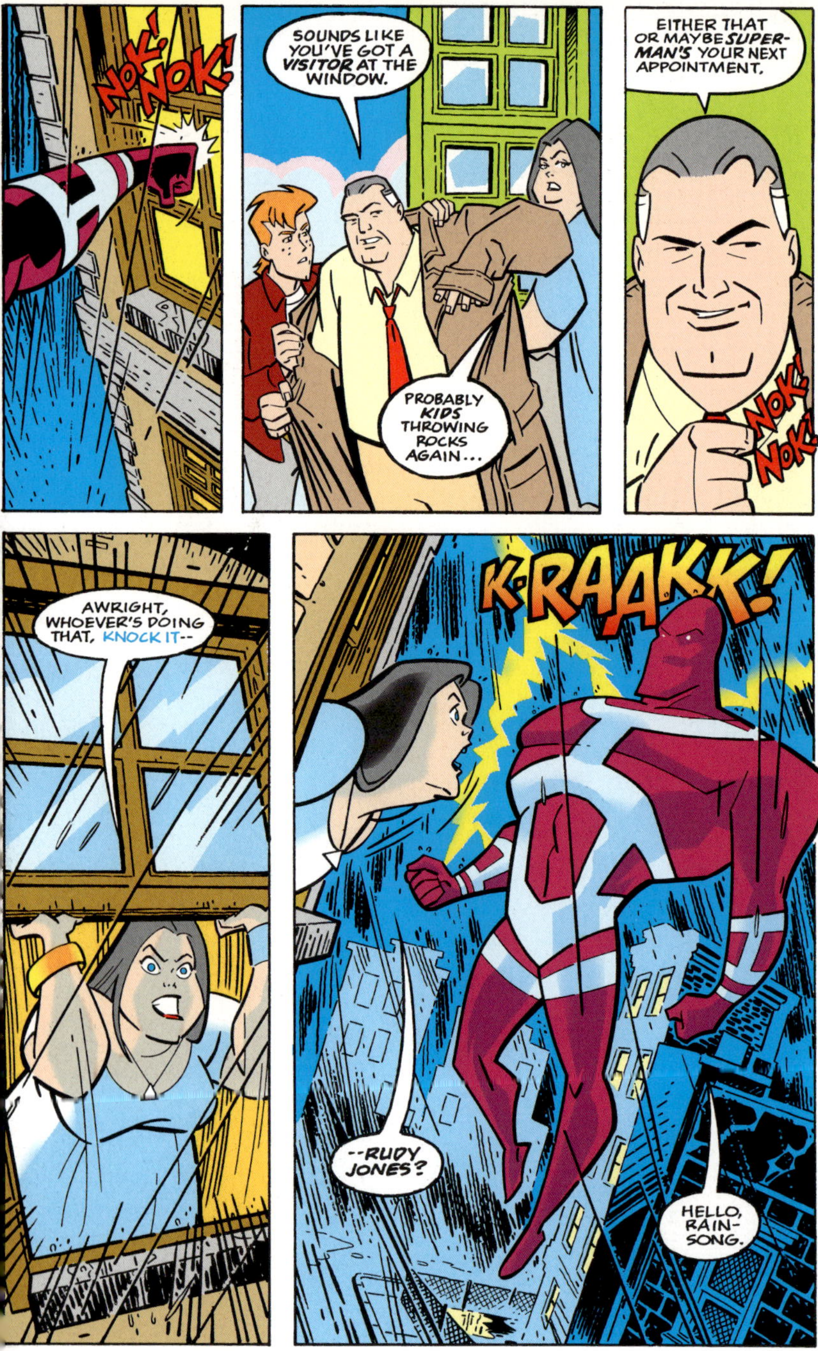
NOK! NOK!
SOUNDS LIKE YOU'VE GOT A ***VISITOR*** AT THE WINDOW.
PROBABLY ***KIDS*** THROWING ROCKS AGAIN...
EITHER THAT OR MAYBE ***SUPERMAN'S*** YOUR NEXT APPOINTMENT.
NOK! NOK!
AWRIGHT, WHOEVER'S DOING THAT, KNOCK IT--
K-RAAKK!
--RUDY JONES?
HELLO, RAIN-SONG.

ATTENTION, ALL UNITS! THE PARASITE HAS BEEN SIGHTED IN SUICIDE SLUM! EYEWITNESSES SAY HE'S KIDNAPPED A RESIDENT...
HE STARTED STEALING WINOS NOW, OR WHAT?
...AND IS CURRENTLY HEADED NORTH.
KEEP YOUR EYES PEELED, BOYS AND GIRLS.
Um, CHIEF, I THINK WE GOT SOMETHING...
PARASITE SIGHTING NEAR THE OLD NUCLEAR PLANT OUTSIDE TOWN, CAPTAIN.
BUCKLE UP AND GET READY FOR A ROUGH NIGHT, PEOPLE. WE'RE MISSING ONE MAN OF STEEL, WHICH MEANS THIS IS A JOB FOR SPECIAL CRIMES.
SORRY, CAPTAIN...

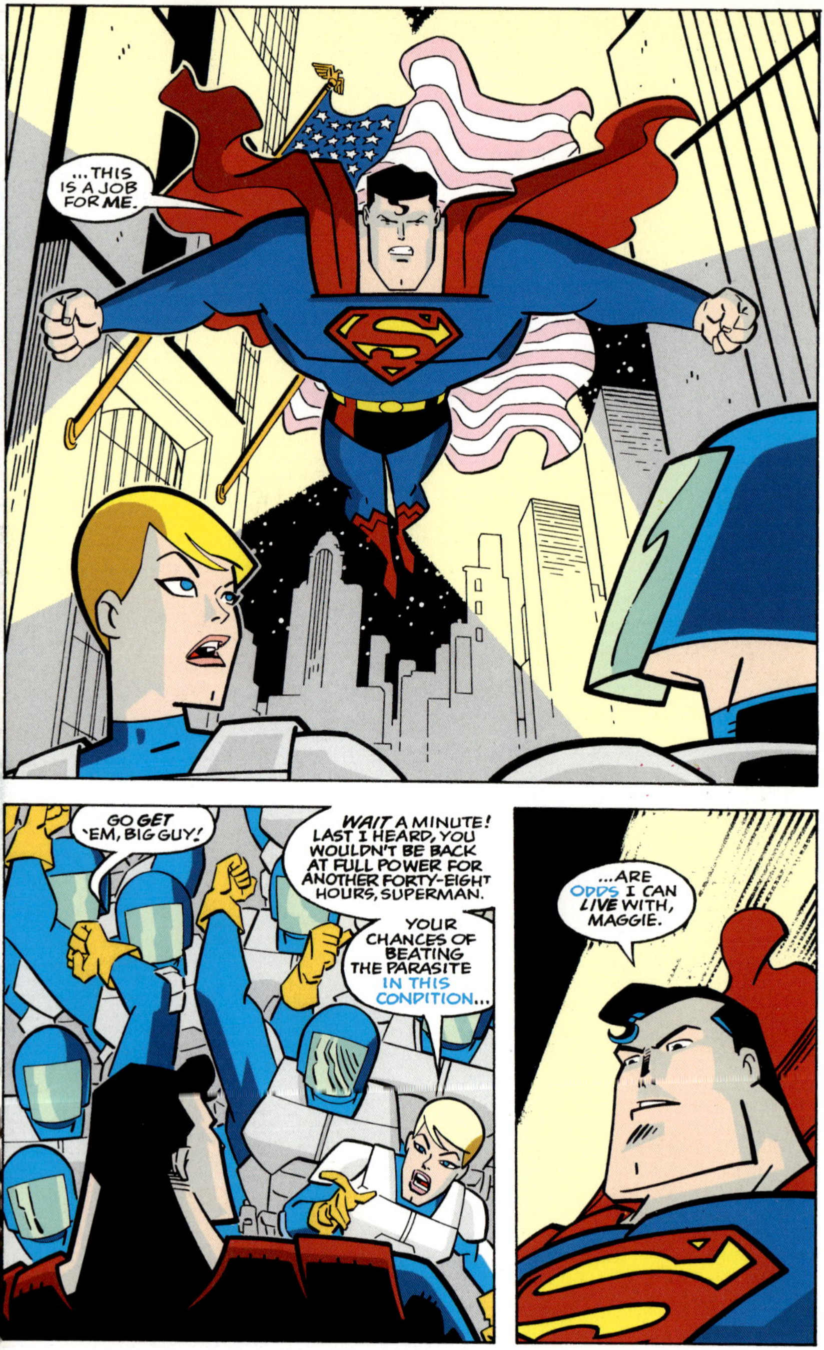
...THIS IS A JOB FOR ME.
GO GET 'EM, BIG GUY!
WAIT A MINUTE! LAST I HEARD, YOU WOULDN'T BE BACK AT FULL POWER FOR ANOTHER FORTY-EIGHT HOURS, SUPERMAN.
YOUR CHANCES OF BEATING THE PARASITE IN THIS CONDITION...
...ARE ODDS I CAN LIVE WITH, MAGGIE.

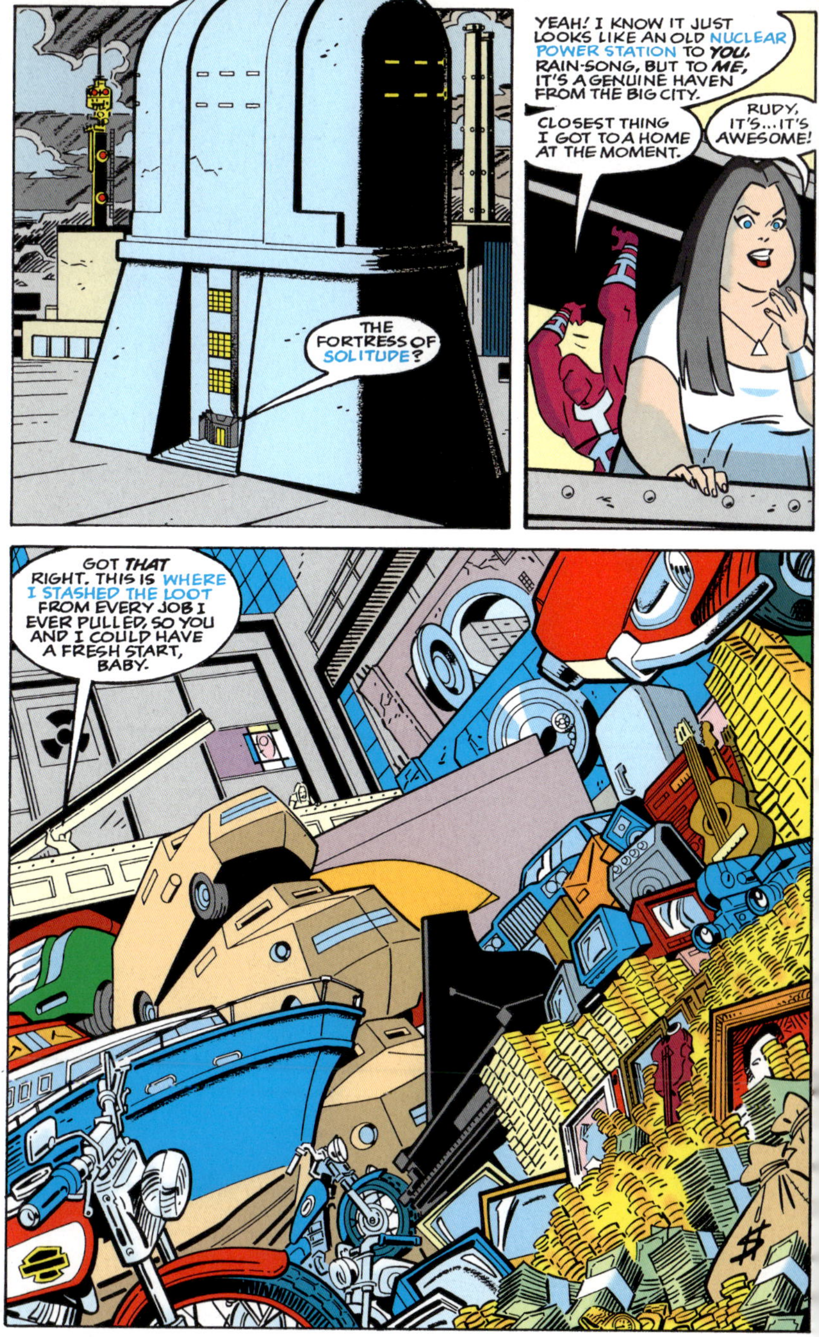
THE FORTRESS OF SOLITUDE?
YEAH! I KNOW IT JUST LOOKS LIKE AN OLD NUCLEAR POWER STATION TO *YOU,* RAIN-SONG, BUT TO *ME,* IT'S A GENUINE HAVEN FROM THE BIG CITY.
CLOSEST THING I GOT TO A HOME AT THE MOMENT.
RUDY, IT'S... IT'S AWESOME!
GOT *THAT* RIGHT. THIS IS WHERE I STASHED THE LOOT FROM EVERY JOB I EVER PULLED, SO YOU AND I COULD HAVE A FRESH START, BABY.

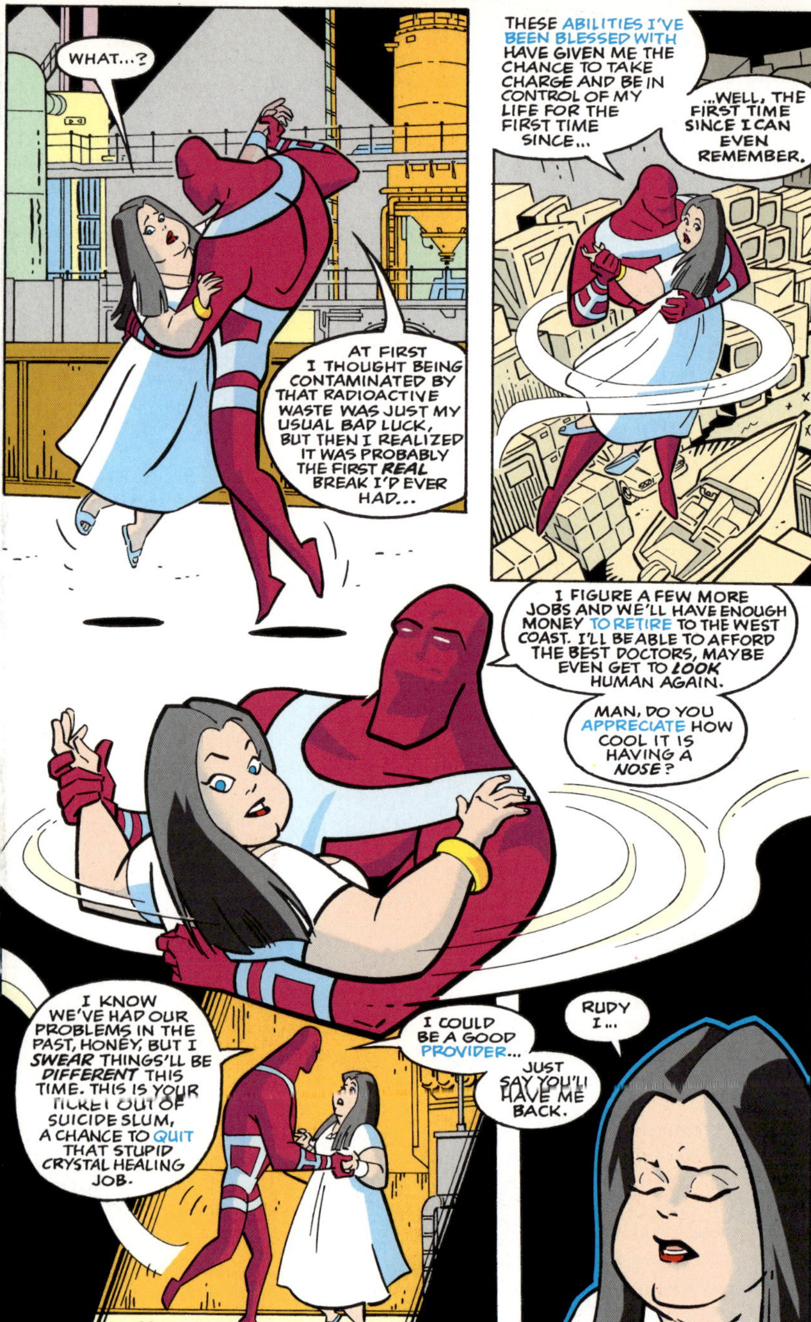

WHAT...?
AT FIRST I THOUGHT BEING CONTAMINATED BY THAT RADIOACTIVE WASTE WAS JUST MY USUAL BAD LUCK, BUT THEN I REALIZED IT WAS PROBABLY THE FIRST REAL BREAK I'D EVER HAD...
THESE ABILITIES I'VE BEEN BLESSED WITH HAVE GIVEN ME THE CHANCE TO TAKE CHARGE AND BE IN CONTROL OF MY LIFE FOR THE FIRST TIME SINCE...
...WELL, THE FIRST TIME SINCE I CAN EVEN REMEMBER.
I FIGURE A FEW MORE JOBS AND WE'LL HAVE ENOUGH MONEY TO RETIRE TO THE WEST COAST. I'LL BE ABLE TO AFFORD THE BEST DOCTORS, MAYBE EVEN GET TO LOOK HUMAN AGAIN.
MAN, DO YOU APPRECIATE HOW COOL IT IS HAVING A NOSE?
I KNOW WE'VE HAD OUR PROBLEMS IN THE PAST, HONEY, BUT I SWEAR THINGS'LL BE DIFFERENT THIS TIME. THIS IS YOUR TICKET OUT OF SUICIDE SLUM, A CHANCE TO QUIT THAT STUPID CRYSTAL HEALING JOB.
I COULD BE A GOOD PROVIDER...
JUST SAY YOU'LL HAVE ME BACK.
RUDY I...

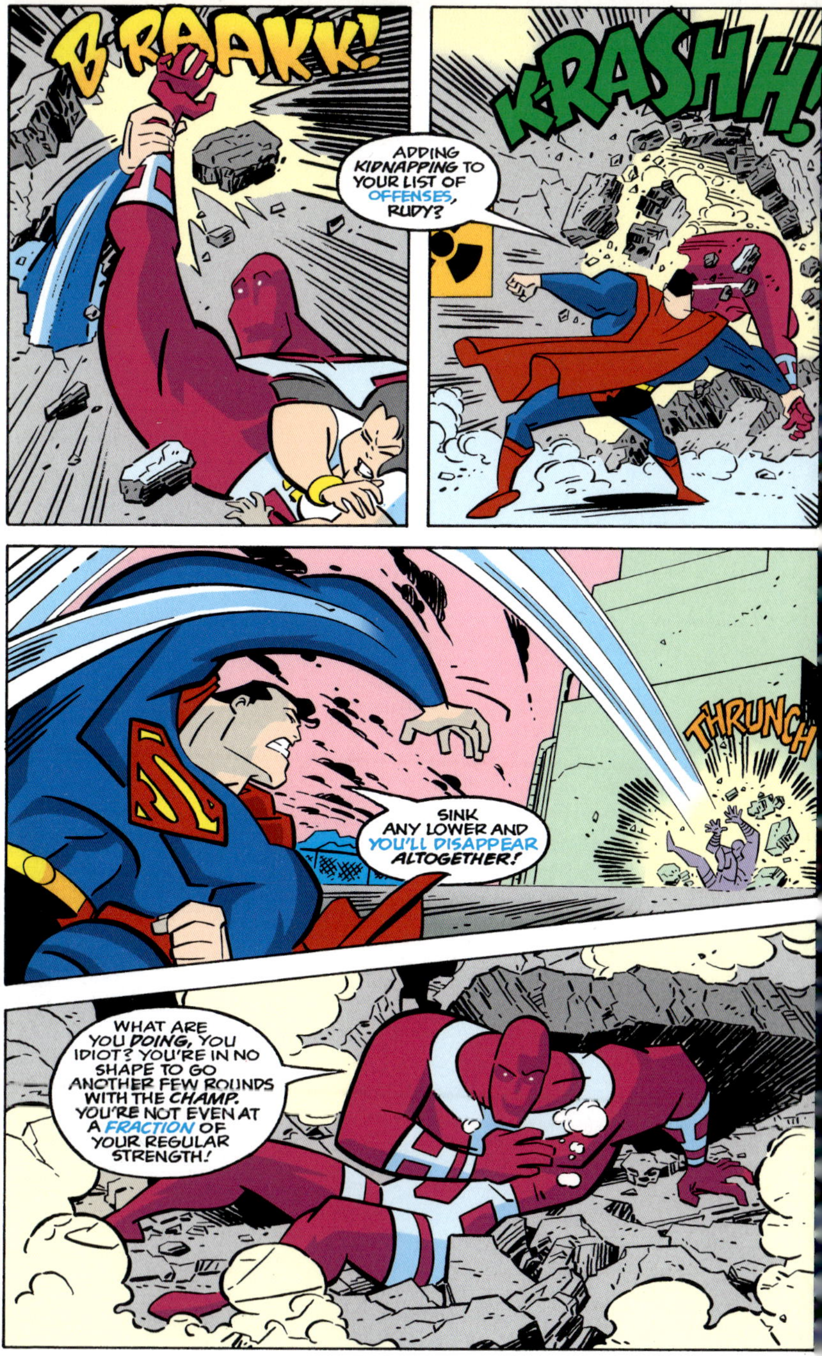
B-RAAKK!
K-RASHH!
ADDING KIDNAPPING TO YOUR LIST OF OFFENSES, RUDY?
THRUNCH
SINK ANY LOWER AND YOU'LL DISAPPEAR ALTOGETHER!
WHAT ARE YOU DOING, YOU IDIOT? YOU'RE IN NO SHAPE TO GO ANOTHER FEW ROUNDS WITH THE CHAMP. YOU'RE NOT EVEN AT A FRACTION OF YOUR REGULAR STRENGTH!

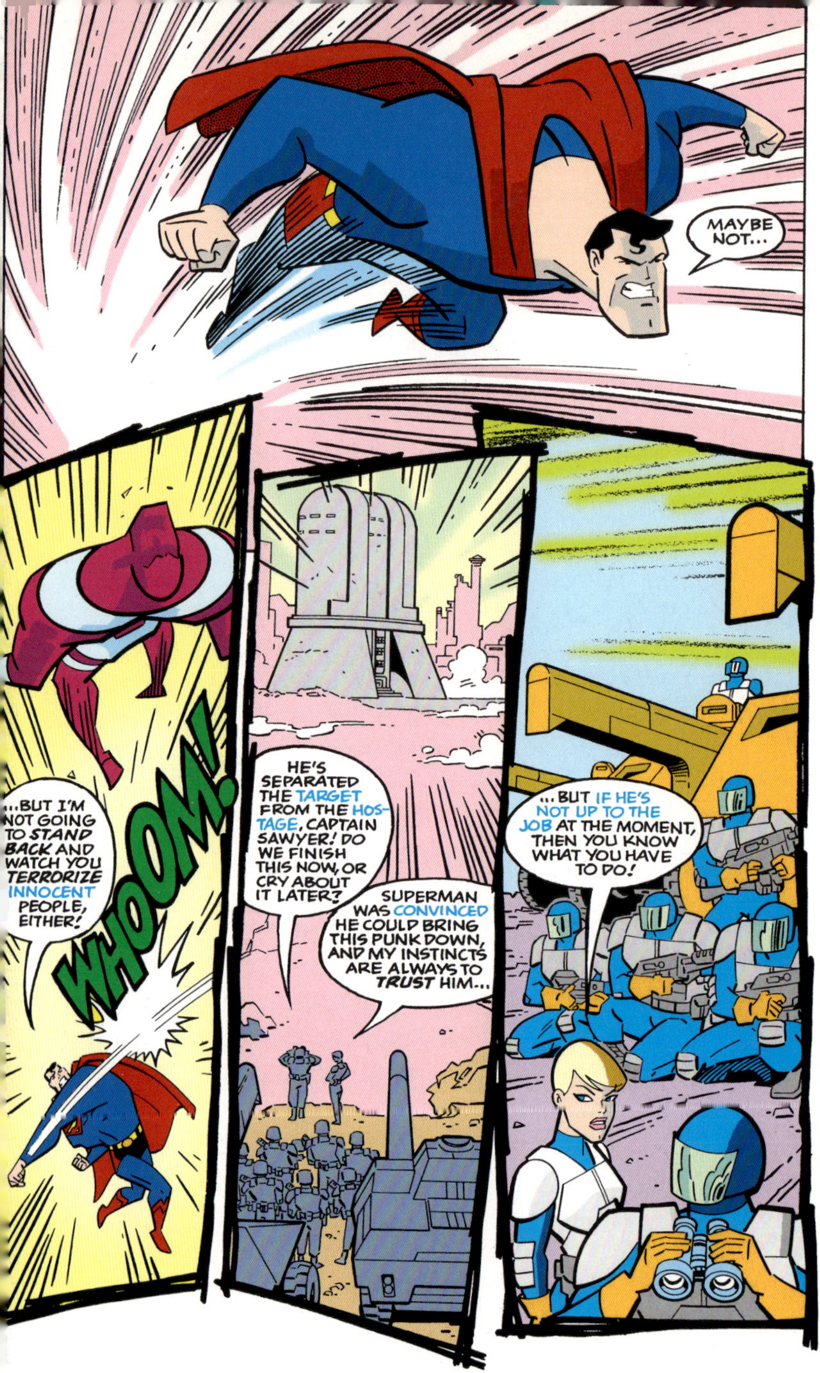
MAYBE NOT...
...BUT I'M NOT GOING TO STAND BACK AND WATCH YOU TERRORIZE INNOCENT PEOPLE, EITHER!
WHOOM!
HE'S SEPARATED THE TARGET FROM THE HOSTAGE, CAPTAIN SAWYER! DO WE FINISH THIS NOW, OR CRY ABOUT IT LATER?
SUPERMAN WAS CONVINCED HE COULD BRING THIS PUNK DOWN, AND MY INSTINCTS ARE ALWAYS TO TRUST HIM...
...BUT IF HE'S NOT UP TO THE JOB AT THE MOMENT, THEN YOU KNOW WHAT YOU HAVE TO DO!

YOU MIGHT BE STRONGER AND FASTER THAN I AM RIGHT NOW, PARASITE...
THOKK
...BUT YOU'VE BARELY HAD FORTY-EIGHT HOURS TO PRACTICE USING MY POWERS.
I'VE BEEN DOING THIS A LONG TIME AND, BELIEVE ME, EXPERIENCE COUNTS OVER MUSCLE EVERY TIME.
NO DOUBT ABOUT IT, SUPERMAN...
Fapp
...BUT I STOLE YOUR EXPERIENCE, TOO.
AAIIGGHH!
Ka-RAASSHH!

WHOOOM
WHAT...?
IT'S THE S.C.U.! I CAN SEE THEM WITH YOUR TELESCOPIC VISION!
THEY'RE GONNA KILL US, SUPERMAN! GET RAIN-SONG OUT OF HERE BEFORE THEY SCORE A DIRECT HIT!
BUT WHAT ABOUT YOU?..?
I CAN'T HOLD THIS RUBBLE BACK MUCH LONGER, SUPERMAN!
SHUT UP AND GET MY GIRL OUT OF HERE!
BOOM

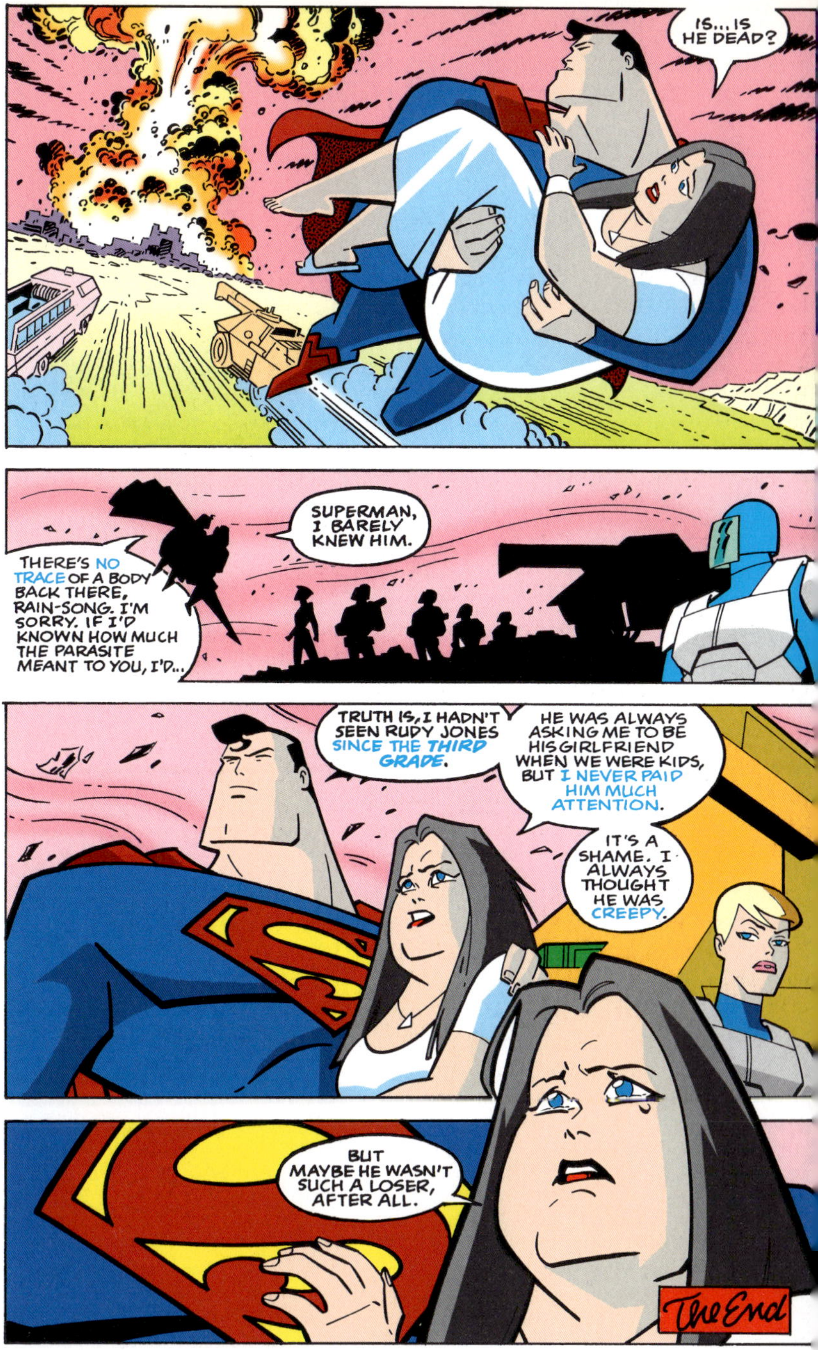
IS... IS HE DEAD?
SUPERMAN, I BARELY KNEW HIM.
THERE'S NO TRACE OF A BODY BACK THERE, RAIN-SONG. I'M SORRY. IF I'D KNOWN HOW MUCH THE PARASITE MEANT TO YOU, I'D...
TRUTH IS, I HADN'T SEEN RUDY JONES SINCE THE THIRD GRADE.
HE WAS ALWAYS ASKING ME TO BE HIS GIRLFRIEND WHEN WE WERE KIDS, BUT I NEVER PAID HIM MUCH ATTENTION.
IT'S A SHAME. I ALWAYS THOUGHT HE WAS CREEPY.
BUT MAYBE HE WASN'T SUCH A LOSER, AFTER ALL.
The End

Inhaltsangaben

Clark Kent, du bist ein Niemand! (S. 5–26)

In der Redaktion des *Daily Planet* sind alle Computer ausgefallen. Clark Kent kann deshalb nicht auf seinen Terminkalender zugreifen und wird das Gefühl nicht los, etwas Wichtiges zu verpassen. Als er von Lois Lane hört, dass ein Passagierflugzeug bei einem Zusammenstoß mit einer kleineren Maschine beschädigt wurde und nun mitten in der Stadt notlanden muss, macht er sich sofort auf den Weg. Beim Sprung aus dem Fenster muss er allerdings feststellen, dass er nicht mehr fliegen kann. Er stürzt hinab – und wird von einem Wesen gerettet, das aussieht wie Superman und anschließend auch das Passagierflugzeug sicher nach Gotham City bringt!

Um zu überprüfen, wie es um seine übermenschlichen Kräfte steht, nimmt Clark Kent an einer Pressekonferenz teil, auf der Professor Hamilton mitteilt, dass der Gesteinsbrocken vom Planeten Krypton zerstört werden soll. Man will verhindern, dass Supermans Widersacher ihm damit Schaden zufügen. Clark berührt den Stein – und nichts geschieht! Er ist also zu einem normalen Menschen geworden …

Während eines Besuchs bei seinen Adoptiveltern in Smallville denkt Clark darüber nach, wer für den Verlust seiner Kräfte verantwortlich sein könnte. Erneut wird er Zeuge, wie ein anderer als Superman auftritt und einen Tornado unschädlich macht.

In der Redaktion funktionieren endlich alle Computer wieder, und Clark kann seine Termine abrufen. Sofort ist ihm klar, wer sich an seiner Stelle als Superman ausgibt. Er ruft den Kobold Mr. MXYZPTLK mit einer Hundepfeife und macht ihn mit einem Trick unschädlich: Er bringt ihn dazu, zweimal seinen eigenen Namen rückwärts zu sagen und schickt ihn damit für weitere 90 Tage in die fünfte Dimension. Sofort kann Clark nun wieder über seine Superkräfte verfügen.

Der Leibwächter aus Stahl (S. 27–48)

Ein Kopfgeld von einer Milliarde Dollar ist auf den Präsidenten der Vereinigten Staaten ausgesetzt worden – vermutlich von Waffenherstellern. Sie wollen verhindern, dass der Präsident ein Friedensabkommen unterzeichnet und ihnen damit das Geschäft verdirbt. Superman testet und durchbricht den Verteidigungsring, der zum Schutz des Präsidenten um das Weiße Haus errichtet wurde, und stellt sich bis zur Friedenskonferenz als persönlicher Leibwächter zur Verfügung.

Der von Lex Luthor angeheuerte Killer ist ein Schurke namens Larry Liebowski alias Multi-Face. Multi-Face ist in der Lage, jede beliebige Gestalt anzunehmen.

Am Tag des Gipfeltreffens wird Lois Lane der Zutritt zum Saal verwehrt, weil ihr Name nicht auf der Liste der zugelassenen Journalisten steht. Lex Luthor bietet ihr einen Platz an seiner Seite an. Als der Präsident ans Rednerpult tritt, überprüft Superman die Sitzreihen und entlarvt Multi-Face, der sich als Clark Kent verkleidet hat. Der Schurke richtet daraufhin seine Spezialwaffe auf Superman, denn er soll in Wirklichkeit ihn umbringen, nicht den Präsidenten. Im letzten Augenblick kann der Leiter der Sicherheitskräfte, General Hardcastle, Superman wegstoßen und so aus der Schusslinie bringen. Lois macht derweil den Bösewicht unschädlich, indem sie ihn mit einem Feuerlöscher k.o. schlägt.

Kriegsspiele Teil 1 und 2 (S. 49–92)

In Metropolis ereignet sich eine Serie gefährlicher Zwischenfälle, die alle auf Fehlsteuerungen in Computersystemen zurückzuführen sind. Superman kann anfangs noch Schlimmeres verhindern, die Situation gerät aber immer mehr außer Kontrolle. Im Keller des Daily-Planet-Gebäudes explodieren sämtliche Computer, und wenig später fällt in der ganzen Stadt der Strom aus.

Gerade noch rechtzeitig kann Professor Hamilton den Nordpol als Ausgangspunkt für die Sabotageaktionen lokalisieren. Superman und der Professor machen sich sofort auf den Weg dorthin. Sie treffen auf den Schurken Brainiac, dem es gelungen ist, aus seinem Gefängnis auszubrechen. Er hat vor, die Erde durch die Zündung aller nuklearen Sprengköpfe zu zerstören und sich mit den in einer Kugel gespeicherten Daten der Erde abzusetzen. Im Zweikampf gelingt es Brainiac, Superman handlungsunfähig zu machen.

In der Zwischenzeit kann in Metropolis wegen des Stromausfalls eine weitere Gefangene entfliehen: Livewire. Lois Lane überredet sie, ihre Kräfte für die Menschen in Metropolis zu gebrauchen. Livewire befreit Superman und opfert sich selbst, um so die computergesteuerten nuklearen Raketen zu stoppen. Brainiacs genialer Fluchtplan wird am Ende von Superman doch noch vereitelt.

Macht verdirbt, Superkräfte verderben noch mehr (S. 93–114)

Superman rettet einem Fallschirmspringer das Leben, der sich allerdings als der Bösewicht Rudy Jones alias Parasite entpuppt und Superman seine Kräfte entzieht. Er benutzt sie dazu, Banken auszurauben und Verwüstung anzurichten. Außerdem entführt er die Heilerin Rain-Song, seine Jugendliebe. Um mit ihr ein neues Leben anzufangen, hat er sich mithilfe von Supermans Kräften die dafür nötigen finanziellen Mittel beschafft.

Als Superman versucht, Parasite aufzuhalten, reichen seine Kräfte nicht aus. Rain-Song setzt sich für Superman ein und macht Parasite klar, dass sie ihn nicht liebt. Die Spezialeinheit, die Superman gefolgt ist, nimmt den Bösewicht ins Visier. Um seine Jugendliebe zu retten, opfert Parasite sein eigenes Leben.

Rätsel und Übungen

Clark Kent, You're a Nobody! (S. 5–26)

1 Wie viele Vokabeln haben Sie sich aus der ersten Superman-Episode gemerkt? Übersetzen Sie die folgenden Wörter mit der Hilfe von SUPERMAN ins Englische. Falls Ihnen ein Wort nicht mehr einfällt, werfen Sie einfach einen Blick auf die entsprechende Ausklappseite.

1 Röntgenblick	5 Terminkalender
2 beleidigen	6 Auftrag
3 Termin	7 bewaffnet
4 tödlich	8 Briefumschlag

1 _ - _ _ _   _ _ S _ _ _

2 _ _ _ U _ _

3 _ _ P _ _ _ _ _ _ _ _

4 _ E _ _ _ _

5 _ _ _ R _

6 _ _ _ _ _ _ M _ _ _

7 A _ _ _ _

8 _ N _ _ _ _ _ _

2 Oft werden Wörter in bestimmten Kombinationen verwendet. Erinnern Sie sich, welche beiden Begriffe jeweils zusammengehören? Verbinden Sie die Wörterpaare:

Jurassic	speaking
combined	currents
emergency	age
air	landing
scientifically	assault

The Bodyguard of Steel (S. 27–48)

3 In diesem Buchstabendickicht haben sich elf englische Wörter aus der zweiten Superman-Episode versteckt. Die Suchbegriffe sind waagerecht (von links nach rechts), senkrecht (von oben nach unten) oder diagonal (von links oben nach rechts unten) angeordnet.

Die deutschen Entsprechungen lauten:

gefährden Verkleidung Versuch durchschnittlich

Ziel fälschen Rückgang

darauf erpicht offen gesagt verrückt Gipfeltreffen

i	b	s	q	p	j	t	a	r	g	e	t	o	w
n	d	f	z	d	a	g	o	u	m	b	a	h	k
s	i	a	x	l	i	c	b	l	a	s	t	y	j
a	c	k	p	o	r	s	e	t	a	j	w	q	e
n	x	e	c	y	b	o	g	i	u	m	p	y	o
e	t	f	g	r	d	e	i	u	c	v	s	l	p
a	a	t	t	e	m	p	t	z	i	w	r	k	a
h	n	m	p	s	l	y	z	g	x	s	b	u	r
u	i	r	n	k	g	c	e	o	t	q	e	d	d
f	r	a	n	k	l	y	p	a	z	w	b	s	i
a	v	t	y	j	w	o	k	d	g	e	z	m	z
p	x	m	s	u	m	m	i	t	p	e	q	y	e
t	d	f	l	v	k	y	r	g	a	b	r	l	o
w	i	q	c	a	n	k	u	s	t	z	m	p	v
b	p	q	e	o	u	a	v	e	r	a	g	e	z

4 Lösen Sie das Kreuzworträtsel, indem Sie die deutschen Begriffe übersetzen.

Die Buchstaben in den markierten Feldern ergeben – richtig zusammengesetzt – den Namen eines Schurken, der Superman Probleme bereitet.

waagerecht:	senkrecht:
1 enttäuschen	3 Zufall
2 Auswahl	4 außer
6 völlig	5 Vorfälle
8 Zusammentreffen	7 freiwillig
9 Stromausfall	10 Verrückter
11 Kurve	14 so tun als ob
12 Atem	
13 Unverwundbarkeit	
15 anständig	

Der Name des Schurken lautet:

☐ ☐ ☐ ☐ ☐ ☐ ☐ ☐

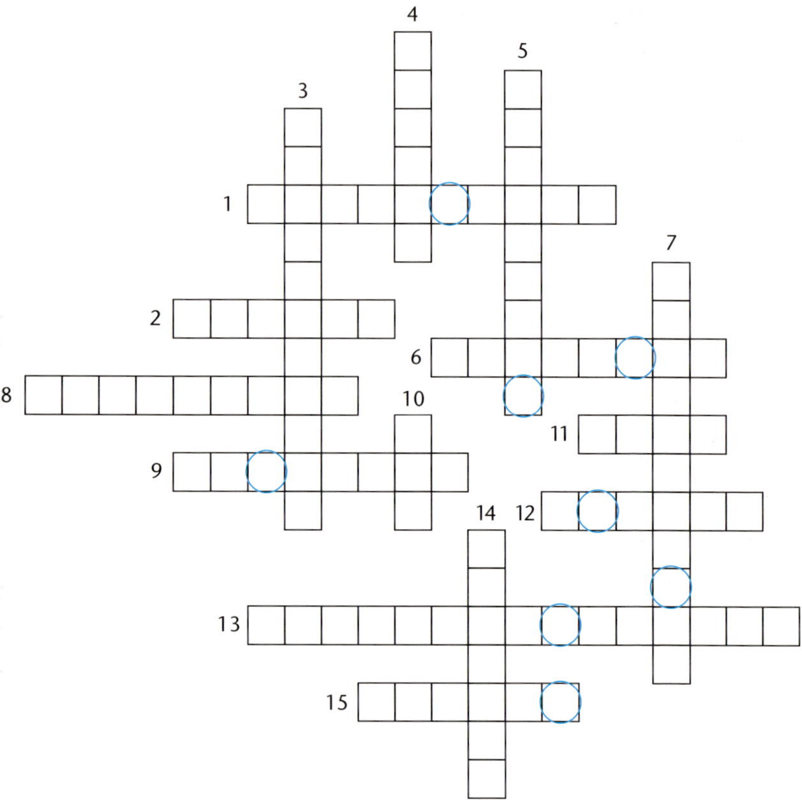

1
2
3
4
5
6
7
8
9
10
11
12
13
14
15

5 Vervollständigen Sie die Sätze mit dem passenden Wort. Es ist jeweils nur eine der angegebenen Möglichkeiten richtig.

The bridge wasn't ________________, so Superman had to lift the ship and fly over it.

out of order | down | raised | cleared

The computer room in the Daily Planet building didn't have any windows, because it was in the ________________.

elevator | power plant | bend | basement

Brainiac said to Professor Hamilton: "You are ________________ your few remaining breaths."

wasting | losing | doing | taking

Livewire ________________ herself to save the world.

rescued | sacrificed | traced | hid

6 Ordnen Sie die unten aufgeführten Wörter nach ihrer Aussprache. Achtung: Zwei Begriffe passen zu keiner der beiden Gruppen!

brakes [äi]	garbage [ah]
________________	________________
________________	________________
________________	________________
________________	________________

awesome crackle raise launch equation
disable calls guardian carriage pray

Power Corrupts. Super Power Corrupts Absolutely! (S. 93–114)

7 Mit diesem Quiz können Sie beweisen, dass Ihnen kein Detail der Geschichte entgangen ist. Nur eine der angegebenen Möglichkeiten ist korrekt. Wenn Sie die entsprechenden Buchstaben richtig zusammensetzen, erhalten Sie Parasites eigentlichen Namen, und zwar den Nachnamen.

1. After rescuing the parachutist Superman promised to take him …
   A … home.
   O … to the football stadium.
   S … downtown.

2. When Parasite stole Superman's powers, the people on the street …
   B … ran away.
   F … called the police.
   S … yelled at him.

3. In order to have time to recover from the attack, Superman told Lois that …
   G … his parents wanted to see him.
   R … he had an appointment with a crystal healer.
   J … he had the flu.

4. How long would Parasite be able to use Superman's powers?
   E Two to three days.
   C 24 hours.
   Y Two weeks.

5. Parasite robbed several banks because he wanted to …
   L … build a huge nuclear power station.
   N … move to the west coast and start a new life there.
   T … buy Lexcorp Corporation from Lex Luthor.

Parasite heißt eigentlich _ _ _ _ _ .

8 Tragen Sie die englischen Entsprechungen der angegebenen Begriffe in die dafür vorgesehenen Felder ein.

```
        O
        O
O   O   S   O   O   O   O   O
        O
        O
        O
        O
→ Bewohner ↓ Geisel

        O
        O
O   O   U   O   O
        O
        O
→ Sprung ↓ vertrauen

        O
        O
        O
        O
O   O   P   O   O
        O
        O
        O
        O
→ Tiefe ↓ verschwinden

        O
        O
        O
    O   E   O   O   O
        O
        O
→ komisch ↓ gruselig
```

O
O
O O R O O O
O
O
O
→ gerade mal ↓ Ziel

O O M O
O
O
O
O
O
→ Drecknest ↓ Schwachköpfe

O
O
O O A O
O
O
→ überspringen ↓ entziehen

O
O
O O O O N O O O
O
O
O
O
O
→ in Gefahr bringen ↓ unschuldig

Lösungen:

1 1 X-RAY VISION
2 INSULT
3 APPOINTMENT
4 LETHAL
5 DIARY
6 ASSIGNMENT
7 ARMED
8 ENVELOPE

2 Jurassic age
combined assault
emergency landing
air currents
scientifically speaking

3

i	b	s	q	p	j	t	a	r	g	e	t	o	w
n	d	f	z	d	a	g	o	u	m	b	a	h	k
s	i	a	x	l	i	c	b	l	a	s	t	y	j
a	c	k	p	o	r	s	e	t	a	j	w	q	e
n	x	e	c	y	b	o	g	i	u	m	p	y	o
e	t	f	g	r	d	e	i	u	c	v	s	l	p
a	a	t	t	e	m	p	t	z	i	w	r	k	a
h	n	m	p	s	l	y	z	g	x	s	b	u	r
u	i	r	n	k	g	c	e	o	t	q	e	d	d
f	r	a	n	k	l	y	p	a	z	w	b	s	i
a	v	t	y	j	w	o	k	d	g	e	z	m	z
p	x	m	s	u	m	m	i	t	p	e	q	y	e
t	d	f	l	v	k	y	r	g	a	b	r	l	o
w	i	q	c	a	n	k	u	s	t	z	m	p	v
b	p	q	e	o	u	a	v	e	r	a	g	e	z

4

1 DISAPPOINT
2 CHOICE
3 COINCIDENCE
4 EXCEPT
5 INCIDENTS
6 ENTIRELY
7 VOLUNTARILY
8 ENCOUNTER
9 BLACKOUT
10 NUT
11 BEND
12 BREATH
13 INVULNERABILITY
14 PRETEND
15 DECENT

Der Name des Schurken lautet:
PARASITE

5 The bridge wasn't raised, so Superman had to lift the ship and fly over it.

The computer room in the Daily Planet building didn't have any windows, because it was in the basement.

Brainiac said to Professor Hamilton: "You are wasting your few remaining breaths."

Livewire sacrificed herself to save the world.

6

brakes [äi]	garbage [ah]
raise	awesome
equation	launch
disable	calls
pray	guardian

7 1. After rescuing the parachutist Superman promised to take him to the football stadium. **O**

2. When Parasite stole Superman's powers, the people on the street yelled at him. **S**

3. In order to have time to recover from the attack, Superman told Lois that he had the flu. **J**

4. How long would Parasite be able to use Superman's powers? Two to three days. **E**

5. Parasite robbed several banks because he wanted to move to the west coast and start a new life there. **N**

Parasite heißt eigentlich (Rudy) J O N E S .

8

HOSTAGE / RESIDENT

TRUST / BOUND

DISAPPEAR / DEPTH

CREEPY / WEIRD

TARGET / BARELY

MORONS / DUMP

DRAIN / LEAP

INNOCENT / ENDANGER